Bob —
What a pleasure!
Our very best — you're one
in a million!
Mary-Ellen

To BOB REES —
To one of the best
I've met in this
great craft of
clubmaking!

Dan
Wishon

The Search for the Perfect Driver

The Search for the
Perfect Driver

Tom Wishon

with Tom Grundner

SPORTS
MEDIA
GROUP®

All inquiries should be addressed to:
Sports Media Group
An imprint of Ann Arbor Media Group LLC
2500 S. State Street
Ann Arbor, MI 48104

Library of Congress Cataloging-in-Publication Data

Wishon, Tom W.
The search for the perfect driver / Tom Wishon with Tom Grundner.
p. cm.
ISBN-13: 978-1-58726-311-8 (hardcover : alk. paper)
ISBN-10: 1-58726-311-4 (hardcover)
1. Golf clubs (Sporting goods) I. Grundner, Thomas. II. Title.

GV976.W583 2006
688.7'6352—dc22

2006023579

Printed and bound at Edwards Brothers, Inc., Ann Arbor, Michigan, USA.

10   09   08   07   06   1   2   3   4   5

ISBN-13: 978-1-58726-311-8
ISBN-10: 1-58726-311-4

Contents

Introduction

Here are two simple truths for you. You can't be a good race car driver without knowing how an engine works, and you can't be a good golfer without knowing how golf clubs work.

Few people would argue with the first part of that sentence. Yet how many golfers genuinely understand how and why golf clubs work the way they do? This is especially true when it comes to the driver. If you don't believe that, let me challenge you with a little experiment.

Go out to your local driving range and, at some point, take a few moments to look around you. Watch the other golfers for a while—especially when they take out their drivers. If you see two or three golfers out of ten who can consistently hit the ball straight, on a nice trajectory, you're there on a good day. I am not talking about hitting 300-yard drives right down the middle. I am talking about the ball flying high and straight, landing downrange at any reasonable distance, within 20 yards on either side of its intended target.

Now, think about what you're seeing. Name any other recreational pursuit in which one of its most common goals seems so unattainable, by so many people.

This is not to say that golf is not a difficult and often frustrating sport. Even at the PGA Tour level you will see shots go awry and the occasional club slammed into the ground. But does that account for what you are seeing at the driving range?

I believe it's safe to say that far less than half of all golfers can consistently get off the tee with a driver successfully—and that's being charitable. Now, imagine any other consumer product that works only half the time in the hands of an average user. A product like that would be off the market in a week; yet we in golf just shrug our shoulders and say, "Gosh, it's a tough game."

I know what you are going to say: "It's not the arrow, it's the archer," and to a certain extent that's true. In my early years as a PGA teaching pro I saw some swings that weren't just bad, they were scary, and it is the rare golfer who could not benefit from a session or two with a qualified instructor. But I am sure that's not the complete answer.

Would you be shocked to learn that each year, literally millions of drivers sold are designed *from the factory* to be unhittable in the hands of the golfers who buy them? That seems hard to believe, but consider this:

The average male golfer shoots a 97. Now, go into your local golf store or pro shop and look at the row after row of 9- or 10-degree, 45- to 46-inch-long drivers. What do you think the probability might be that someone who shoots a 97 (or greater) could possibly control a 45- or 46-inch-long club, let alone control it and generate the swing speeds necessary to make that 9- or 10-degree loft work? Heck, for that matter, what do you think the probability is of someone who routinely shoots in the 80s doing it? Let me give you a hint. The average driver length on the PGA Tour in 2004–2005 was 44.5 inches. These are the best golfers in the world. If they felt they could control a 45- or 46-inch club, they would; they can't, so they don't. Yet that is the option being commonly presented to YOU at virtually all retail golf stores and golf course pro shops—and most people, even the retailers who sell the clubs, unfortunately don't know enough about clubs to know why that driver length will probably not work for them.

Let me give you one more example. In a survey taken at the 2006 AT&T Pebble Beach Pro-Am tournament on the PGA Tour and reported in *Golf World* magazine, the average driver loft of all the professionals participating was 9.2 degrees. The average driver loft of the pros' amateur partners, the majority of whom would have had a handicap north of 12, was 9.4 degrees. Knowing so well how loft has to be matched to the golfer's swing speed, and knowing that in no way did the amateurs' swing speeds even come close to their professional partners', we see a classic example of how misinformation in the marketing of golf clubs is truly preventing golfers from being all they can be when they step on the tee with that No. 1 in their hands.

Let me emphasize one thing: I am *not* saying that you can buy your way into being a great golfer. No golf club, by itself, can turn you into that. I am saying, however, that equipment that doesn't fit—that is the wrong length, or loft, or weight, or balance for the way *YOU* swing—can keep you from being all that you could be as a golfer (at any level), and it might even keep you from becoming a golfer at all.

And that's where the real misfortune lies.

Each year something like three million people *leave* the game of golf. When they are surveyed as to why, one of the most common reasons given is "frustration with the game." Yes, the game can be frustrating; I've already pointed that out. But how much of that frustration can be attributed to equipment that not only does not, but *cannot,* meet the golfers' needs? Thinking they are playing with equipment that is properly designed and fitted (after all, they paid enough for it), they can then ascribe their failings only to themselves—to their own ineptitude—and give up on the game. You can see it in their eyes when they come off the course. It's as if they were saying: "That is the *last* time I am going to be embarrassed like that in front of my friends!"

Approaching this from the standpoint of counting existing golfers, drawing from recent statistics, there are about 27 million Americans who play golf. Of that number, a little more than 12 million are considered "core golfers," i.e., the people who play more than eight times a year and who drive the golf economy. Over the past several years, many of these core golfers have become increasingly disenchanted with the golf club business. In an effort to keep pushing sales, big companies are now bringing out new models every year instead of every two to three years, each introduced with the usual hoopla promising better performance than the last model. When golfers see the driver they bought for $400 in March become a $200 close-out in October of the same year to make room for the next new model, some are beginning to think that maybe these companies are more interested in their credit cards than in their golfing performance. As a result, a large and growing segment of core golfers in America are looking for different options for getting better performance from their equipment investments.

If you don't understand how club length, the loft angle of the face, the flex and weight of the shaft, and the weight balance of the club all have to be properly matched to the way you swing, the club remains simply that—a club, in the Cro-Magnon sense of the word. You will continue to buy those 9- or 10-degree, 45-inch drivers and be mystified as to why you can't hit them solid and straight more than half the time. You will continue to experience frustration with a game in which your only real objective is to have fun.

In 2005, along with Tom Grundner, I wrote a book called *The Search for the Perfect Golf Club*. To my semi-amazement, it became a best seller. I knew there was a need for such a book, but did not anticipate the level of demand.

We're back with a variation on that theme to help golfers make far better informed club-buying decisions.

The Search for the Perfect Golf Club was a comprehensive overview of all clubs. It was the first book to explain to the layman how and why golf clubs work the way they do. When they don't work, it explained the likely reasons and what you can do about it. It introduced the concept that *all* golfers—but especially middle- and high-handicappers and yes, beginners—should have clubs that are custom fitted. And, among other things, it told you what to look for (and look out for) when buying clubs—custom fitted or otherwise.

The Search for the Perfect Driver is in some ways a subset of that previous book, but in some ways it goes well beyond it.

To begin with, it focuses on only one club—the driver. In the first section, it will explain the technology behind the driver—how and why it works the way it does, and so forth. It's intended to be a buyer's guide for your driver so your tee shot game can be the best that it can possibly be . But then it goes a step further.

The second section makes a very important point. *The golf swing is as it is, because the golf club is as IT is*. Indeed, the two are inextricably tied together. When buying golf clubs with little knowledge of what we need, we all too often swing the club the way we do because the club is designed the way it is. In other words, if the driver does not fit, it can definitely force the golfer into making some poor swing moves. But the corollary to that is this: by changing the characteristics of the club, we can change the outcome of the swing and in the process end up with golf clubs that match up far better to the way each individual golfer swings.

To prove my point, I take a series of common swing problems and show you, step by step, how equipment modifications can help with each one. Indeed, in many cases, faulty equipment might have been the *cause*. This is not meant to be a substitute for lessons, but if lessons are not in the cards, a custom club or custom alteration should be.

In both sections of this book I've tried to keep things light and interesting. First, I've used a Q & A format so the book will seem more like a conversation and less like a textbook. Second, I have limited the discussion to the things you need to know to end up with the best club ever to live in your golf bag under the headcover with the number 1 on it. This book is not intended to be an exhaustive treatment of these topics; for more information on anything you see here, I urge you to pick up a copy of *The Search for the Perfect Golf Club*.

Finally, you'll notice early on that I am continuing the theme which I began in the first book, namely, that golfers at all levels—including beginners—*need to have clubs that are custom fitted*. That's not a real popular idea among the mass-market club companies whose business model it is to make and sell millions of standard-made clubs, but it's true none the less. As you read this book you will see why.

The point of both books, however, is the same. Golf is about having fun. These books are about understanding its tools and removing some of the barriers that keep it from being more fun for more people.

Enjoy and learn!

Tom Wishon
Durango, Colorado

Part I
The Wonder of It All

1 | A Head Start

All right, I am a perfect example of what you're talking about in your introduction. I've never been completely happy with my driver, and I know next to nothing about golf clubs. What do I do now?

Well, you've already taken an excellent first step—you bought this book.

You say you can't hit your driver as well as you'd like. There are only three possible reasons for that. Either there is something wrong with your club, or there is something wrong with your swing, or the laws of physics are somehow magically suspended on the golf course when you play. Let's rule out the third possibility, shall we?

That means the problem is either in your club, or in your swing, or both—meaning they don't match up well with each other. The concept of a properly fitted driver, or *any club* for that matter, is that the club is made to fit *your swing*, not that you change your swing to be able to swing the club.

Wait a minute. I am not going to blame my club. It's a big-name popular driver, and a lot of golfers use the same one. How could that be the source of the problem?

I am well aware of the popularity of some of the heavily marketed standard-made drivers that are bought off the racks in retail pro shops and golf stores. The question I am raising is: what did you buy?

If I ever decide to get out of the golf business, I think I am going to open up a running shoe store based on the same business model as a retail golf store that sells the heavily marketed, brand-name golf clubs. I will have hundreds of shoes to choose from, but all of them will be the same size—9½ for men, which is about their national average, and 7½ for women, which is about their average shoe size. If your foot happens to be a 9½ or your wife's a 7½, all well and good. If it doesn't, wear them anyway. After all, it's not the shoe; it's the runner, right?

When you buy a driver off the rack, you are buying a club that has been designed and assembled to some kind of national average—or worse, made to what the marketing mavens believe the majority of you and your golf friends will be receptive to. When you put on a pair of shoes, you can immediately tell if they don't fit. With a driver, or any other golf club for that matter, most people can't. They hit a high percentage of bad tee shots and automatically assume it's their swing that's the cause. With shoes you've learned over a lifetime what to look for and look out for. Most golfers can't even begin to do that with their clubs.

Okay, where do we start?

Let's start with some terminology. That way, as we talk about this stuff later, we'll have a common framework of understanding. And if you happen to know all this terminology stuff, don't boot me out yet; there's a *whole lot more* to come that I bet you don't know about drivers. So, bear with me here for a second as we begin the journey to find *your* perfect driver.

Every driver head has three basic parts: the *hosel* (pronounced HAW-zul), the face, and the body. The hosel is the neck of the clubhead. It's where the shaft goes in. (Yes, I know, several Callaway brand drivers don't have a hosel, but let's not worry about the few exceptions for right now.) The *face* is the surface that strikes the golf ball, and everything else is called the *body.*

The body is further divided into the *heel* (the end closest to the hosel), the *toe* (the end farthest from the hosel), the *sole* (the bottom of the head), the *skirt* (the part that curves all around the sides of the head), and the *crown* (the top of the head). On most heads you'll see a little plastic ring at the top of the hosel. That's called a *ferrule* (FAIR-ul), but it has no real function except as a

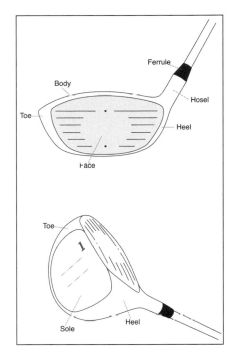

While clubhead designers have a wide vocabulary when referring to specific clubhead parts, the above terms are the minimum that the average golfer should know.

decoration. No, it won't keep your graphite shaft from breaking. It's just a decorative piece to that connects the appearance of the hosel smoothly to the surface of the shaft.

The face of every club (not just the driver) is tilted back from the golf ball to a certain extent. That tilt is called the *loft angle*. In addition, every hosel is also tilted more upright or back toward the golfer to a certain extent, and that's called the *lie angle*.

One more important thing and we're done (for right now).

Ever set a driver down to rest on the ground and noticed that the face didn't point straight down the fairway? That's the *face angle*. The driver head can be designed to have an open, square, or closed face angle. If you haven't seen much in the way of different face angles on drivers, that's probably because the big standard club companies pretty much make all their drivers with one and only one face angle, namely a square-to-very slightly closed face angle. Remember what I said about standard clubs for average golfers? Face angle is one of the very average things on most drivers today.

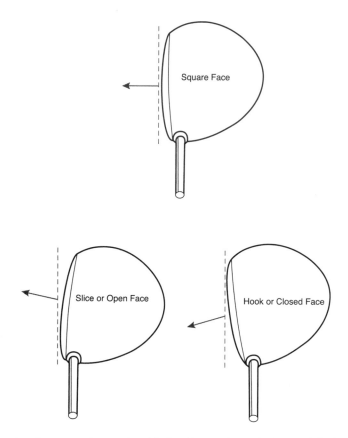

Choosing the correct face angle with the driver and woods is one of the best examples of how custom fitting can offer real game improvement to any golfer with accuracy problems.

Which of those terms is the most important to know about in buying the right driver for me?

Far and away, the two things in the driver head that are going to influence your game the most are loft and face angle. There are other factors that will also influence it, especially in the assembly specifications of the driver, but we'll get to those a bit later.

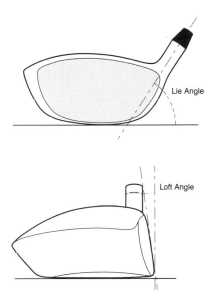

The loft angle is the angle between the face plane and a vertical plane running perpendicular to the sole of the clubhead. The lie angle is the angle between the axis of the hosel and the ground line.

Let's start with loft.

As I just stated, loft is the extent to which the face of the driver is tilted back away from the golf ball. When you go into a golf store, 95 percent of the men's drivers they have in stock will have lofts ranging from 9 to 11 degrees. What the store guy will probably not tell you, because he simply does not know, is that a lot of golfers today need *more loft on their drivers to hit the ball farther.* Here's why.

The loft angle controls the launch angle, the speed at which the ball leaves the face, and amount of backspin imparted to the ball. This is important because how far you hit the ball is all about those three things. The ball speed and the backspin are also determined by how fast you can swing the driver, but the launch angle is not. No matter whether you swing the driver at 50 or 150 mph, the launch angle remains the same; it is a product of the loft and of whether you swing upward toward, level with, or downward toward the ball. The height of the shot is certainly different for golfers of different swing speeds, but that is a different matter than the launch angle. The same launch angle flying up at 150 mph is certainly going to achieve a much higher trajectory and height than at 50 mph. But the launch angle will be the same for any swing speed as long as the loft and angle of attack are the same. What is usually not mentioned is that the loft of the club *must be matched to your swing speed and something called your swing angle of attack,* in order to get maximum distance.

Remember I just said that the launch angle was determined by the loft and by whether you swing upward toward, level with, or downward toward the ball? That swing approach is called the angle of attack, and it is determined by your swing. If you tee the ball farther forward, flex your wrists forward at impact, or "fire and fall back" when you swing, you probably have an upward angle of attack. If you make a downswing similar to the way you chop wood or lunge forward as you swing, you likely are delivering the clubhead to the ball on a more downward angle of attack. In between is the level angle of attack, where the clubhead is moving toward the ball parallel to the ground.

If you want to really see what the angle of attack can do to the flight of the ball, just go find a gentle mound out on your golf course. If you hit some shots from the upslope side of the mound, you'll notice how much higher you hit the ball with whatever club you use. Now take the same club, head over to the downslope, and watch the height of the shots you hit. That's an example of what a downward angle of attack will do to the height of the ball. We custom clubmakers make it a goal to identify your angle of attack and then pick the driver loft that matches with your swing speed to milk every possible yard from your swing speed.

Wait a minute. I thought the lower the loft the farther the ball will go.

Yup, that's true … with your 5-wood, 7-wood, and your irons. Even with the obscene swing speeds of John Daly, Tiger, or Bubba Watson there is a point at which the driver loft will be too low for them to generate their longest driving distances. Sure, for them it

Level Angle of Attack

Downward Angle of Attack

Upward Angle of Attack

The angle of attack describes whether your swing delivers the clubhead to the ball on a downward, level, or upward path. It is a critical element in the selection of the best driver loft to maximize your distance off the tee.

might be the low single digits of loft, but for the rest of us mere mortals, to get more distance you will probably need a HIGHER loft, one that is definitely double digits and quite possibly a number with a "teen" after it. I know that sounds counterintuitive, so let me explain it this way.

I'm sure that at one time or another you've played around with a garden hose. Imagine you have the hose turned on full blast and you are trying to get as much distance as possible out of the water spray. Now, suppose someone turns the water pressure back by about a third. You can feel the pressure drop in your hands and see the loss of distance in the spray. So, what do you automatically do to try to get that distance back? Exactly! You raise the angle of the nozzle.

It's the same way with the driver.

If you have a very fast swing speed (i.e., the hose is on full blast), you need a lower loft to get maximum distance. If you have a slower swing speed (i.e., the hose pressure has been cut back), you need a *higher* loft to get more distance. *What you MUST NOT do is match a slow swing speed with a low-lofted driver.* That is the equivalent of lowering the water pressure *and* lowering the nozzle angle, and then wondering why the water isn't going as far.

So, how fast can you reasonably expect to swing your driver *with control*? Here are some numbers that might give you a sense of where you probably fall. I've listed some average driver swing speeds and included a chart that shows the average *carry distance before the roll of the ball* with drivers of different loft. By knowing your *accurate carry distance* you can work backward to estimate your driver swing speed.

Average Female Golfer: 65 mph

Average Male Golfer: 87 mph

Average Female Tour Player: 97 mph

Average Male Tour Player: 110 mph

Male Long Drive Competitors: 135–155 mph

Female Long Drive Competitors: 105–120 mph

Now couple the results with the following. To get the maximum distance out of a 9- or 10-degree driver, you need a swing speed (with control!) of about 110 mph. The rest of us (in the 80, 90, and 100 mph speed ranges) will get maximum distance for carry plus roll from 11- up to 15-degree clubs. Golfers with a swing speed lower than 80 mph won't begin to reach their maximum potential distance for carry plus roll with less than 15, 16, or 17 degrees of loft. I kid you not. Perhaps you are one of many who hit your 3-wood as far as or farther than your current driver and wondered why. Well, now you know one of the main reasons.

Carry Distance in Yards Before Roll

Swing Speed (mph)	Driver Loft 9°	Driver Loft 11°	Driver Loft 13°	Driver Loft 15°	Driver Loft 17°
50	57	65	72	77	81
60	91	102	109	115	119
70	131	142	149	153	156
80	170	179	184	186	187
90	205	211	213	213	211
100	234	237	236	234	230
110	258	258	254	249	243
120	277	274	268	261	253

Note: Carry distances are based on a level angle of attack into the ball. An upward angle of attack requires a little less loft than that shown in the chart above, while a downward angle of attack will require more loft for each swing speed than that shown in the chart above.

Think about that the next time you walk into Mad Mike's Golf Emporium and Fashion Boutique and see row after row of 9- and 10-degree drivers on the rack. You think those clubs are designed for YOU?

Okay, I got it. The driver head needs to be at the correct loft. But you also mentioned this swing thing called the angle of attack. How's that involved in my finding the best driver?

Let me use those gorillas of the grass, the long drive competitors, to explain that. If you've ever watched a long drive competition on TV, you might have noticed that they show the competitors' launch parameters for most of their shots. Most all of these guys generate a 12- to 13-degree launch angle to hit the ball that far, but they do that with a driver that has 6, 7, or 8 degrees of loft. Now think about those numbers in relation to each other. A 6-degree loft driver causing the ball to fly off the face at an angle of 12 degrees? The *only* way that can happen is if the golfer is swinging the clubhead *upward* to hit the ball. That comes from the swing and a forward ball position, and that's what is called an upward angle of attack.

For *all golfers* there is a launch angle that will be just like that perfect match of the angle of the garden hose with the force of the stream: a perfect launch angle combined with the golfer's swing speed and the loft of the driver head that will get that ball to fly as far as the golfer's swing speed can mash it out there. Now, here's the trick the long drive people know and use to their advantage. If you can get close to that optimum launch angle from an upward angle of attack in your swing, you can then use a lower loft on the driver head and still reach that perfect launch angle for your swing speed. The less loft you can use on the driver head and still get that ball up to the right launch angle for *your* swing speed, the more ball speed you will generate, and the lower the backspin will be. For these busters of the ball with their 135–155 mph swing speeds, high ball speed and low backspin is the way they creep up to that 400-yard line out in that logo-emblazoned, floodlit fairway on which they compete. And the way they get that is to train their swings so they have a more upward angle of attack.

For most of us slappers of the surly sphere, it's pretty much the same way, except for the backspin part of it. The more we can get to our perfect launch angle by swinging on an upward angle of attack, the less loft we have to use. The lower the loft we can use and still reach our perfect launch angle with the help of a more upward angle of attack, the farther we all could hit the ball. No question. This is one reason some of the PGA Tour players are actually developing a totally different swing to use with the driver than with any of the other clubs. Because distance is rewarded so much on the PGA Tour, many of these guys are learning how to hit the driver on a more upward angle of attack than they will use when hitting any other club in their bag.

So you're telling me I need to go out and change my swing to hit more up on the ball? I thought you were just telling me that I need more loft to hit the ball farther with a driver!

I was. Remember, these aberrations of human anatomy who rip it out there 400 yards have one really important distance thing that you, I, and 99.9 percent of our fellow fanatics don't have ... a tremendously high swing speed. They also are pretty darn good athletes, at least from the standpoint of being able to make the slight swing change that will *consistently* deliver the clubhead on a slightly more upward angle of attack. Again, the reason you are a businessman, and I am a clubmaker, and the two of us are not playing this great game for a living is that our golf swings are weak and our bodies can't swing the club that fast—at least in comparison to the tour players and the national long drive competitors.

All of us need to find an optimum launch angle that will squeeze out all the distance we have in our swing speed after being matched with the right driver loft angle. And seriously, for about 90 percent of the golfers who play this great game, that means they should not try to mess with changing their swing. They should just use more loft on the driver than they currently use. For the other 10 percent, with the athletic ability to control a swing change and the time to internalize it, by all means go for a slightly upward angle of attack with the driver. It's what a lot of the tour players have done and are doing.

So, the driver head needs to be at the correct loft. But why is the face angle so important?

Very simple. If your driver face angle is wrong for your swing, you're going to be suffering in terms of how many times you keep the ball on the short grass versus the rough or trees. Or maybe I should say that if your driver face angle is matched correctly to your swing, you have a real good chance to boost the number of fairways you hit and the number of holes you can play with a ball before you lose it.

Here's the deal.

Obviously, to make the ball go straight, the driver head should be traveling straight down the target line with the face pointed directly at the target when it hits the ball. Most of us don't and can't do that the majority of the time, because somewhere along the line in our golf swing training, we have developed an errant swing path and/or can't seem to get our arms and hands to deliver the clubface square to the ball and to the target. The result is the noxious array of curved shots we view with all-too-familiar disdain. The clubheads on the vast majority of drivers sold standard off the rack are designed with a square or a very slightly closed face angle, with closed meaning that when you set the driver down to let the clubhead rest flat on its sole, it looks like the face is pointing a little to the left (and that would be pointing a little to the right for you left-handed players).

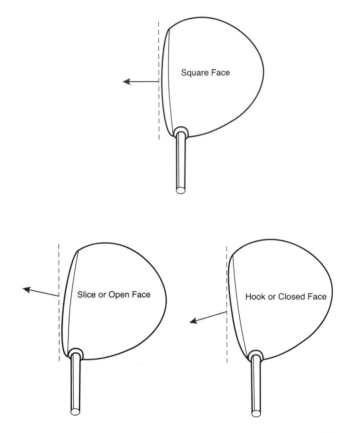

Custom fitting the face angle of the driver to the misdirection tendency of the golfer is one of the most powerful of all clubfitting specifications for improving the accuracy of the tee shot. This is a driver design option that is virtually nonexistent in standard-made driver heads purchased off the rack and typically can only be fitted and provided by a skilled custom clubmaker.

All of that is well and good, but my problem is that I SLICE it to the right—and badly at times, too.

Ah, yes, the dreaded slice. The bane of so many golfers the world over.

This is a perfect example of what I meant when I said you can't buy your way into being a good golfer. There is no such thing as a club that will absolutely keep you from slicing the ball. There are, however, design features you can ask for that will certainly help minimize the problem and keep you in play a lot more often without having to change your swing. That's where the face angle I just talked about comes in, along with another driver-design feature called offset.

I explained that the vast majority of driver clubheads are produced from the head-making foundries so the face will point straight at or very slightly to the left of the target when you line up the club. That's true, but it's not true for *all* drivers. Let's go back to the beginning.

If you are slicing it's because, for whatever reason, you are not getting the clubface square to the target line at the instant it hits the ball. The driver head is coming through the ball with the face slightly open, which is causing the backspin rotation on the shot to tilt a little sideways, which causes the ball to curve to the right.

The face on a driver head with a *closed face angle* is not lined up straight to the target line. It is turned to the left (to the right in left-handed driver heads) and can be designed to turn anywhere from 1 to 4 degrees. So, let's say you have a swing flaw that causes you to come through with your clubface 2 degrees open, thus causing your slice. If you have a driver with a 2-degree-closed face angle built in, the face will now present itself as square when it reaches the ball. Goodbye, slice. Or, let's say you have a more severe swing flaw and your driver face is 6 degrees open at impact. With a 4-degree-hook face angle on the driver head, at impact the face will be open only a net 2 degrees. You'll still fade the ball, but it won't be nearly as bad, and you won't lose as many balls.

Offset is a little more subtle.

Normally the hosel, and by extension the shaft, extends up from the heel side of the driver head with the face well in front of the shaft. In an *offset* clubhead the hosel has a slight curve designed in it so that the shaft is positioned, in effect, *ahead* of the face. This allows your hands and arms an extra split second to get the face around to be less open without you ever having to do anything different in your swing. It doesn't sound like much, but it can really have an effect.

By far the best ways to correct or limit a slicing problem are by having a driver head with either a closed face angle or an offset

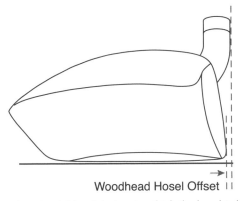

Woodhead Hosel Offset

Offset is the term given to clubhead designs in which the hosel is located ahead of the face. This feature allows the golfer to have slightly more time to rotate the clubface back to square, which reduces the tendency to slice the ball.

hosel, or, if the slice is more severe, having both features together on the same driver head. If you really do slice the ball, what you don't want to waste your time with is one of these fancy drivers with the screws on the outside of the head that allow you to move weight into different places around the head. These drivers are for golfers who only fade or draw the ball and wish to alter that flight a little. They are definitely *not* for golfers who slice or hook the ball.

It is possible to *slightly* change the curvature on the shot by moving weight around the head. Move more weight to the heel side of the head, and you can slightly reduce the amount of fade on the shot. Put that extra weight over on the toe side of the head, and you will be able to slightly reduce the amount of draw that may be naturally present on the shot because of your swing. But if your fade is not a real fade, meaning that the ball curves more than 10 or 15 yards as it flies toward the houses or white stakes, then you are going to be far, *far* better off with a driver head that has a more closed face angle than your current driver, an offset hosel design, or both together on the same head.

All right, I see what hook-facing and hosel offset are all about and how they might help, but I have noticed that all drivers are made with a curved face. If you want to hit the

ball as straight as possible, shouldn't drivers be made so the faces are flat?

Actually there are *two* different curves on the faces of driver heads. When you look at your driver head as you set it down to address the ball, you will notice that the face is curved from the heel to the toe, horizontally across the face. That is called *bulge*. If you look at the face from the side, you will see that it also curves slightly from top to bottom. That is called *roll*.

The bulge is the horizontal radius on the face of every woodhead. Its purpose is to start the ball a little further off line when the shot is hit off center as a means of balancing the sidespin put on the ball from the "gear effect" of the off-center hit.

Bulge Radius

The purpose of bulge is to help keep you in the fairway when you can't hit the ball in the center of the face. It works like this.

If you had a clubhead with a perfectly flat face, and you were to make contact with the ball right on the sweet spot and with the face square to your target line, the ball would go straight. No problem. However, if you hit the ball even a fraction toward the toe side of the face, the head will twist, and the ball will go sailing off to the left. Hit the ball with a totally flat-faced driver a little toward the heel side of the center of the face and the ball will snipe to the right. With bulge, if you hit it a fraction off center, a nice little correction takes place that allows the ball to end up in a much better place.

Let's pretend both the clubface and the ball had teeth—like gears. Let's say the ball makes contact with the clubface toward the toe. The clubhead would then twist back slightly in response to being hit off center. As it did, the "teeth" of the clubface would begin sliding along the "teeth" of the ball, causing it to generate a hooking sidespin.

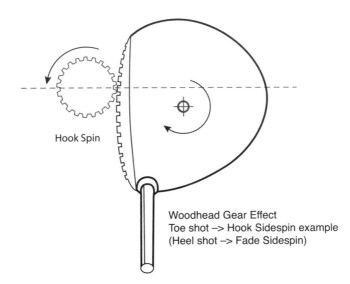

Hook Spin

Woodhead Gear Effect
Toe shot –> Hook Sidespin example
(Heel shot –> Fade Sidespin)

When the ball is hit off-center, the woodhead will rotate. The friction between the ball and the clubface then causes the ball to develop a "hook spin" from a toe shot, or a "fade spin" from a shot mis-hit off the heel. The purpose of the bulge is to start the ball off a bit more to the side so that when the hook or fade spin occurs, the ball will end up back in the fairway.

As a result of the toe-to-heel curvature we call bulge, on a toe shot the ball will start out more to the right because the bulge curvature makes it do that. The hooking spin created by the "gear effect" from a toe shot will help curve the ball back in toward the fairway. The same thing happens (only in reverse) when the ball is hit near the heel.

The clubhead also has that other curvature up and down the face called *roll*. To be honest with you, I've never figured out what the heck the vertical roll radius up and down the face of a woodhead is supposed to do. It's just there. I do know that in recent years, it has become a bit of a problem.

A few years ago, when the trend in driver heads was toward a smaller size, the up-and-down roll radius on the face had little effect on play. But each year, the clubhead has gotten bigger and the face has grown taller. Driver faces that were once 1.5 inches tall are now as tall as 2.5 inches. This increases the face area that is in play when you strike the ball, and the up-and-down roll curve now has a very definite effect.

In the world of club design, loft on woodheads is measured only in the very center of the face. If you have a large-size 11-degree driver with a 2.5-inch face height, and you hit the ball on a spot about the size of a thumbtack in the center of the face, you will get your 11-degree loft. If you hit above it, the up-and-down roll radius raises the loft to as much as 14 degrees. If you hit below the center, it could be a mere 8 degrees. Way back when driver heads had faces that were only 1.5 inches tall, this loft increase and decrease because of the vertical roll radius were not such a big deal. The up-and-down roll radius on a 1.5-inch tall face didn't allow the loft to be much higher on the top of the face or much lower on the bottom of the face.

Club designers are now starting to wake up to this problem. Or at least this one has. Recently I issued my first "wake-up call." It's called a GRT (graduated roll technology) face design. My drivers all have bulge, as they should, but the up-and-down roll curvature is nearly flat. I would think (and hope, for golfers' sake) that soon the other designers will be following suit, but until then, you (or your clubmaker) will have to look for this feature. Because of the great reduction in the vertical face radius, the loft of the woodhead is far more consistent up and down the face, which means that the launch angle at which you hit the ball will be a lot more consistent. And you know the importance of hitting the ball with a consistent launch angle, don't you?

So that means if I use a long tee these days with my jumbo driver head, and tee it up high, I might be hitting the ball up on the top of the face, where there is more loft than what the driver was designed to have?

Bingo! Do you remember a few years ago when a famous-name teacher who does commentary on one of the TV networks was saying that the "hot spot" of all the large drivers is above the center of the face? Several of the golf magazines picked this up and made a big deal out of this. If your definition of "hot spot" on the face is the place where the ball leaves the face with the highest ball speed, that spot is *only* directly in line with the center of gravity inside the head and as with the center of the face where the COR (coefficient of restitution) is the highest.

The reason most golfers hit the ball farther when they make contact above the center of the driver is that most golfers buy too little loft on their drivers to begin with. When they tee it higher with the long tees that have become popular since the advent of big 460cc driver heads, they hit the ball up there where the vertical roll radius puts more loft on the face. One fool proof way of knowing whether you bought too little loft on your driver is to hit the ball dead center in the face; if it doesn't fly as far as when you hit it higher on the face, you have too little loft.

But here's the funny thing about that. If all golfers were to *buy* the right loft on their drivers to get them to their optimum launch angle for a dead-center hit, that dead-center hit would also deliver a higher ball speed. That means they would hit the ball a little farther than when they just hit the ball high on the face with the driver they bought with too little loft! And if they had the right loft to begin with on a driver with reduced roll, then their margin for error in hitting the ball in the center is widened because the loft won't change much up and down the face. See, you have to think about these things.

Most golfers do buy too little loft on their drivers, so when they tee it high and hit it high on the face, they do get more distance than if they hit that same driver in the center of the face. But they lose what they could get if they had the right loft to begin with.

I've heard a lot about something called the "sweet spot," but I have no idea what that is.

It's a term that's commonly found in golf club ads and commonly misused by almost everyone in the golf industry.

You frequently see ads boasting that this club or that has a "larger sweet spot." Technically that can't happen because the actual sweet spot (officially known as the center of percussion) is a point that's about the size of the sharp end of a pin. It can't get "larger," it can't get "smaller." It just … is.

If you deliver the face of the club square to impact and hit the exact center of the golf ball directly in line with this tiny spot, the ball will fly straight, true, and at the greatest distance your swing speed, angle of attack, loft, and resulting launch angle can muster. Any deviation toward the heel or toe from this perfect contact and the head will start to twist, not only imparting sidespin to the ball, but also causing a loss of distance. The farther your point of contact is from this tiny sweet spot, the more distance you lose and the more sidespin you gain.

When club companies talk about an "increased sweet spot," what they are really saying is one of two things. One, they've done things to the clubhead's design to increase the *moment of inertia* (MOI) of the clubhead. In other words, they can put weight all around and/or in the back of the head to make it twist a little less when you miss the sweet spot. Less twist from an off-center hit and you lose less distance. The second one involves the design of the face itself. You probably know by now that big driver faces made from titanium flex inward when you hit the ball. The more you can flex the face, the higher your ball speed will be in relation to your swing speed. But here again, if you miss the center of the face when you make contact with the ball, that face can't flex as much, and you start losing distance.

By making the outer edges all around the whole face a little thinner than the center, it is possible to make the face flex a little more when you hit the ball off center and not lose that much distance. The most typical version of this type of face design is to make the face a little thicker in an oval-shaped area in the center of the face, but then thinner in the areas all around that thicker center oval area. But, no matter what, if you miss the center of the face, the face cannot flex as much, and there will be some distance loss. A well-engineered thick-center/thin-outer face can slightly reduce this distance loss for each off-center hit increment.

How do you know whether you're buying a driver head with a high MOI or a more forgiving face design? By listening to the company's ads ... uh, as long as the company is really telling the truth and not describing their driver MOI and face design like that fish your kid told his uncle he caught last summer.

Wait a minute. You're saying I am losing distance every time I don't hit the ball on the sweet spot?

Absolutely!

Golfers will spend hundreds of dollars on a new driver in hope of hitting the ball an extra five to ten yards. What they don't understand is that you can get that added distance and more with your current club simply by hitting closer to the sweet spot more often.

Look at the test data. Let's assume you normally hit your driver 200 yards on the fly. If you hit it one-half inch off center toward the toe or heel (either way), you lose roughly 10 yards; three-quarters of an inch, 15 yards; and so forth.

A lot of people can hit their 3-wood off the tee as far as, if not farther than, their driver. Part of it has to do with the 3-wood's loft being more appropriate to their swing speed, but much of it has to do with the 3-wood's length being significantly shorter than that of the driver. Because the club is shorter, it is easier to control the club when you swing. The more you have control of the club, the more likely you are to hit at or near the sweet spot. Just doing that alone will get most golfers back all the distance they *think* they are losing by using the 3-wood in the first place.

A minute ago you used the term "moment of inertia." Now there's a term I've heard before but do not really understand.

You might not have heard of it, but it has a *huge* effect on how well you will hit that driver of yours. Let me explain it this way.

Have you ever watched a figure skater doing a spin? When the skater's arms are out, his or her moment of inertia (i.e., resistance to twisting) is increased, so the skater spins more slowly. When the skater's arms are drawn in close to the body, the moment of inertia is immediately decreased, so the skater spins faster. In other words, low moment of inertia, less resistance to twisting— high MOI means it's more difficult to twist the object.

Well, the same thing happens with the golf clubhead. The clubhead's natural resistance to twisting (moment of inertia) can be increased if the designer puts extra weight out at the heel and toe, and also by moving some as far back behind the clubface as possible. The more the designer can do that (i.e., extend the clubhead's "arms"), the more resistance to twisting you have, and the "larger" (i.e., more forgiving) the so-called sweet spot will be.

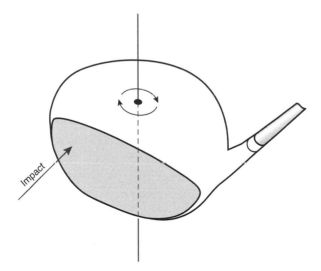

The amount the head twists around an axis straight through the center of gravity in response to an off-center hit is determined by the clubhead's moment of inertia (MOI). The higher the MOI of the head, the less the head twists and the higher the ball speed will be from the off-center hit. Moving more of the head's weight around the perimeter of the head increases the clubhead's MOI.

But no matter what, hitting the ball off center with the driver will result in a noticeable drop in distance.

Everyone these days seem to be playing with heads made of titanium or some other exotic material. Are they really worth the extra expense?

At one point or another, drivers have been made from nearly everything—wood, steel, plastic, aluminum, graphite, titanium, and even ceramics. Along the way, the marketing geeks decided they had free rein to tout almost any nonwooden object as the "next greatest" substance for crafting the driver. If the material was harder than wood, it had to hit the ball farther, right? Well, the answer is no, but that didn't slow down the marketers a bit.

The vast majority of driver heads today are made from steel or titanium because clubhead designers have learned that those metals possess the "right stuff" in terms of strength with some elasticity for its density (what it weighs per volume area). But even within these families of head materials, there is a wide variety of different steel and titanium alloys, and yes, each one represents yet another opportunity for the marketing mavens to spin their promises of greater performance.

As a result, there are a lot of myths floating around concerning the metallurgy of the clubhead. Here are two of them:

The harder the metal, the farther you will hit the ball. And,
The harder the metal, the more difficult it will be to "work the ball" (hit intentional fade and draw shots).

Both statements are wrong. Clubhead hardness has *nothing* to do with how far the ball will travel. It might affect how easily your club gets banged up in the bag, but distance? No way. And there are all sorts of research studies to prove it.

As for the hardness (or lack thereof) affecting your ability to work the ball flight, again, there is no way. Workability (the ability to intentionally fade or draw the ball) is all about the club's *design*. How is the weight distributed? Where is the center of gravity? What is its moment of inertia? How is the face thickness designed? These have nothing to do with the type of metal being used.

What's this I've heard about "spring effect" and COR and all that? Didn't Callaway make some drivers that were actually illegal?

What a can of worms that was ... and, in some ways, still is. Let me start with some background.

In golf there are two major institutions that control what your golf clubs will look like and how they will play; the golf club manufacturers and the United States Golf Association (USGA). The problem is that, by definition, they are on opposite sides of the ball.

The golf club manufacturers (in theory, anyway) want to design clubs that make the game as easy to play as possible. That is the surest way to attract customers and make money. The USGA, on the other hand, controls the rulebook, and their job is to make sure that the golf clubs do not take the challenge out of the game. They want to make sure that technology does not replace skill. Occasionally these two objectives collide, and the results can range from silly to disastrous.

In the mid-1990s titanium drivers were taking the market by storm, and some people were complaining to members of the USGA's Executive Committee that these new exotic metal drivers were hitting the ball too far. They said the clubs were "taking the challenge out of the game." Well, saying those words to the USGA is like waving a red flag at a bull; you just *know* that something is going to happen, you just don't know what.

The USGA looked into it with dark glasses on and found, sure enough, that the average driving distance on the PGA Tour had increased by some 25 yards over the previous 25 years. Never mind that the titanium driver had only been out for a few years, or that the average swing speed of the pros had increased a lot during this time. There were also other factors that could account for that increase, but no matter, the USGA decided to act. So they changed the rules of golf.

In 1998, the USGA revived an old rule that read, "The face shall not act like a spring," a rule that had no scientific definition. The USGA devised a measurement for the coefficient of restitution (COR) to limit the "spring-face effect" of drivers. The USGA decreed that no golf club could have a COR greater than 0.830. In other words, if the USGA shoots a golf ball at your driver head at 100 mph, it better not come back at them any faster than 83 mph, or your driver is "non-conforming."

Wait, you've lost me here. I am not sure I understand why this Coefficient of Restitution number is so important.

Let me explain it this way. When the clubhead and the golf ball collide, the ball squashes against the face, and the face flexes inward. This double compression results in a loss of energy, with the ball, by far, losing the most. Anything you can do to cause the ball to compress less (like allowing the face to flex a little more) will result in less energy loss from the ball, and greater ball speed off the face. This translates into more carry distance at the rate of about 1.8 more yards for each 1 mile per hour more in ball speed.

Because titanium alloys can have such an outstanding combination of strength plus elasticity, titanium-faced woods would flex inward more, thus allowing a higher ball speed coming off the face and more distance than the smaller, thick-faced stainless steel woods of the 1980s and early 1990s. A test for determining the COR of a driver was devised, and the COR limit of 0.830 was written into the books. Things then got *real* interesting.

Okay, what happened then?

Well, along came the giant Callaway Golf Company which saw the rule as an unfair roadblock to their club design capability. Putting on the gloves, Callaway decided to market a nonconforming driver with a COR higher than the 0.830 limit and let the public decide what they wanted. Battle lines were drawn. Callaway complained about the USGA; the USGA complained about Callaway; pundits complained to each other about the sanctity of the rules; and lawsuits were hinted in all directions.

Upon further review (but not by the USGA), it was found that a nonconforming club in the hands of a very high-swing-speed player would gain maybe 7 to 8 yards. It certainly was not the 25 yards that the USGA was blaming on "high-tech equipment." But what was even more interesting was that while the USGA and Callaway were arguing, the Europeans were putting the matter to a practical test.

The Royal and Ancient Golf Club of St. Andrews, Scotland (the R&A) writes the golfing rules for the rest of the world outside the United States and Mexico. They did not enact the same COR limit for their rules as did the USGA for ours. Without a COR limit in effect, any high-COR "over-the-line" driver could be used in any competition outside the United States and Mexico, including all the European PGA Tour tournaments. And you know what happened? Only four of the Euro Tour pros used such high-COR drivers in competition for that whole season. Why? Because the clubs made it more difficult to keep the dang ball in the fairway.

You see, more distance also equals more problems with accuracy, because the same swing error is magnified over the increased distance the ball flies. In the hands of the average weekend golfer, frankly, it would do little or nothing, because the average golfer does not have a high enough swing speed to fully flex the face at impact with the ball. Eventually, the USGA successfully lobbied the R&A to adopt the COR limit for drivers, largely because the USGA wouldn't back down, and it looked bad to the golfing world if the two rule-making bodies disagreed.

Almost all the drivers I see on the racks these days have really huge heads on them. What will one of those oversized heads do for my game?

Nothing.

Nothing?

Well, that's not completely true. It could very well *hurt* your game.

The original idea behind the oversized head was this. If you had a bigger face area you could get a greater "spring-face" effect, thus giving you more distance. But when the USGA put the handcuffs on the maximum COR measurement for a driver, the possibility of increasing driver head size to make the face "spring more" was eliminated.

So now when we designers make bigger and bigger driver heads, we have to make the faces thicker to prevent them from generating a ball speed that would exceed the USGA's rule for spring-face effect. And that, my friend, cancels out any possibility of bigger heads being markedly better than a slightly smaller one.

But wouldn't the bigger head be more resistant to twisting—the moment of inertia thing and all that?

Yes, a larger head might have more resistance to twisting, so if you are currently playing with a wooden driver head or any metal driver smaller than 350cc, you could get four or five more yards from your off-center hits. Anything beyond that point will never show up as distance improvement for off-center hits *strictly from the larger head size*. The reason is that there is one other big thing that controls how far you hit the ball when you make contact off center—the design of the face itself.

Remember I mentioned that there is something called a *variable-thickness* face design? Some, not all, variable-thickness faces on drivers can actually increase the amount of flex the face gives you when you hit the ball slightly off center. So again, because none of the golf shops will take too kindly to you wanting to cut one of their drivers in half to see the design of the back of the face, you have to either "test drive" the head or go to a good clubmaker's shop, where he or she may have experience with a lot of different driver head models and would know which ones have a "hotter face."

There is a second MOI in driver heads which has a bearing on your ability to deliver the face to the ball in a square, open, or closed position. The first MOI we've been talking about is how the head twists horizontally around its own center of gravity when you hit the ball on the heel or toe. The other MOI that's important is how much resistance to twisting there is for the head about the shaft. If you slice the ball, a driver head with a high MOI about the shaft can make you slice the ball more. The high MOI about the shaft means your same exact swing now delivers the face a touch more open to the ball. Unfortunately, the bigger the head size, the larger this MOI about the shaft will typically be.

That's what I mean when I say that a large head could possibly be bad for your game, and that's why you're starting to see that you're going to need a custom fitting professional to sort out what driver is best for YOUR game.

So, a super-sized driver has *no* redeeming value?

Well, it could. The problem is that you will never know if your club has it.

We talked earlier about how people with slower swing speeds need to have a higher launch angle on their shots. Remember the water hose analogy? Well, the bigger the driver head, the more the center of gravity can be moved back from the face, and the farther back that is, the higher the trajectory will be. So, if you don't want to try and locate a 13- or 14-degree driver, just get an oversized head that has had *a lot* of extra weight placed rearward, thus moving the center of gravity *a lot farther* back. You'll be amazed at how much easier it is to hit.

The problem is that, short of sawing the clubhead in half, there is no way of knowing whether that has been done. Sure, the marketing people might tell you that a clubhead has a "more rearward center of gravity," but does it? "More rearward" is a relative term. Remember, these are some of the same people who, a few years ago, put "pimples" on the outside of a driver head and told you (with a straight face) they would increase your swing speed.

Aww, come on, there has to be some advantage to the biggest driver heads, or else they wouldn't be selling as well as they do.

One of the easiest marketing tasks is to make people fall in love with something that is bigger. Bigger is always better, right? Seriously, nothing is automatic in the realm of performance simply because you have a 460cc driver head. It is eminently possible to design a driver head of 350cc and larger that can perform as well as or better than the vast majority of 460cc heads. But it's also eminently possible to design a 460cc head that performs better for off-center hits than a 350cc-size head. The problem is, you and all of your fellow golfers simply don't know which one really is better because the marketing claims typically get in the way of the absolute truth. Let me spell out all that a big driver head *can and can't do* as compared with a smaller one.

Officially it can't have a higher COR from its larger face, because the USGA's rule won't allow that. On the other hand, if you play simply for fun, there are some big drivers out there that you can find and play with that do take advantage of what that larger face can offer. Yes, they're nonconforming, but there are golfers who just want to play for enjoyment, so what the heck. Let 'em. In this case, the bigger head can offer more distance.

It is true that just about any 460cc driver will have a higher MOI (moment of inertia) than about any 350cc head of the same weight. But that MOI increase will never be enough to deliver a marked increase in distance from an off-center hit. In the realm of the "Ifs," it is possible to design a big 460cc head with a face that can deliver a marked increase in distance from off-center hits, but only if the designer is really good at engineering a greater flexing of the face away from the center. No guarantee there unless you are in the know.

And the best way to be in the know about your driver head selection is to do the Allstate thing: put yourself in the hands of a good custom clubmaker who has years of experience in grading and fitting driver heads to his or her customers. Clubmakers can choose from literally hundreds of different driver heads of all sorts of face designs, MOI types, CG location, loft, face angle, and weight. The good clubmakers learn which combinations of these things work best for which types of golfers. There, my friend, is how you could come up with a larger driver head that really could perform better. Or a smaller one that can perform really well too!

My buddy recently bought something called a "hybrid" club. He loves it! Is that something I should look into?

How shiny are your 3-, 4-, and even your 5-irons? Technically, a hybrid is supposed to be a type of club that hits the ball the same distance as a long iron, even though its clubhead might look like that of a chopped-off wood. The hybrid clubhead is thinner than a wood but fatter than the ironhead it is supposed to replace. Since it is fatter, the center of gravity (CG) is farther back from the shaft, and the resulting shot trajectory could be a little higher than that of the normal, thinner-bodied ironhead with identical loft.

But any in-depth discussion of hybrids will need to wait until we get around to writing *The Search for the Perfect Irons*. I am not trying to duck your question; it's just that to really understand how hybrids work, you really need to know a bit more about the physics of the iron, and we will get to that in a future book. Or you can go back to *The Search for the Perfect Golf Club* and read more about them. For now, in the midst of a driver discussion, do this. If you want a hybrid to truly replace some of the hard-to-hit longer irons in your set, just make sure the hybrids have the exact same loft and exact same length as whatever iron you want to replace. Do that, and you'll have a more useful encounter with hybrids as a long iron replacement and not a duplicate of your fairway woods.

I've been looking at some drivers that are not brand names. I guess they're clones. Is it all right to go with one of those?

Whoa, let's start by defining some terms here.

If by a "clone" you mean a club with a head that is literally an identical copy of another clubhead, then: NO, IT IS NOT ALL RIGHT. Any number of club companies will sic their lawyers on the companies that sell these heads in a heartbeat. Secondly, those heads are almost universally junk. If you had the ability, as I do, to measure their tolerances for loft and lie, the integrity of the materials used, and the quality with which they are put together, you would be shocked at what you found. I know you can get those clubs at a fraction of the cost of some other clubs, but trust me, you are getting even *less* than you are paying for.

On the other hand, if you mean you are looking at clubheads with a different shape or style than you're used to, and whose names you don't routinely see on the pages of the golf magazines or on PGA Tour visors and caps, then that's a different matter. What you might not realize is that among those unknown brands are some of the world's finest golf clubs. You might have never heard of them, but the people in the club industry certainly know who some of these companies are.

Let me give you a bit of insight into the golf club business.

To begin with, virtually no clubheads are made in the United States. Almost all of them are made in Taiwan, mainland China, or some other southeast Asian country. The number of foundries that are capable of producing high-quality clubheads is finite; there are maybe 10 or 12 such factories among the 50 or so head production facilities in the world. Every *reputable* golf club company has their heads made at one (or more) of those "good" foundries. Whether you are talking Callaway, Titleist, or Taylor Made, or whether you are talking about my company, Tom Wishon Golf Technology, *the heads come from the same places*. They are made by the same people, using the same materials, to the same standards, on the same machines.

There are two factors that separate the elite from the common in this business. The first is the quality of design. The finest head designs in the world do *not* necessarily come from brand-name, mass-advertised, mass-marketed companies. I will, for example, stack up any Wishon clubhead against any brand-name head, any day, any time, anywhere. The difference is that we are not a mass-market company—neither is Rolls Royce. The reason for that has to do with the next factor.

The second factor is the care and skill with which the club is put together, *relative to your specific needs,* and that is where the brand names, inherently, fall short. My clubs, and the clubs of many other companies similar to mine, are not made a hundred thousand at a time to the same specifications. They are made *one* at a time, to *your* specifications, by a good custom clubmaker. They are not "one size fits all"; they are "one club, one customer, one clubmaker."

Don't get me wrong. There is nothing wrong with buying a Chevrolet. There *is* something wrong, however, if you buy a Chevrolet when you could have bought a custom-built car for the same price or less.

All right, so I understand a lot more about the driver head. If I get one with the right loft, face angle, MOI, and CG features for my swing, then I am pretty much home free, right?

Not quite. You can choose a clubhead that is perfect for your swing characteristics, but if you choose the wrong shaft to go with it, you might have wasted your time and money. So, let's take that up next.

2 | Shafts, Grips, and Stuff

All right, clue me in about shafts. More terms to start with, right?

That's right. Let's get on some common ground here.

When golfers who are in the know talk about shafts, there are some terms you hear come up again and again: weight, flex, torque, and bend profile. But don't panic; this stuff is easy.

Let's start with the basics. A shaft has two ends—a thin end and a thicker end. The thin end is called the *tip*, which is obviously inserted into the clubhead, and the larger end over which the grip is installed is called the *butt*. (Don't you love these high-powered definitions? Hey, you veteran players stay with me; I have a lot more for you guys coming up!) In between, shafts have a *tip section, center section,* and *butt section.* We use these terms to help describe how a shaft's stiffness can be varied over the length of the shaft to create shafts which hit the ball a little higher or lower.

There are four major specifications of a shaft: the shaft weight, flex, torque, and bend profile. To start with, the shaft's weight is the number-one factor controlling the total weight of the club.

Total weight is measured in grams or ounces. The driver head has much less effect on the total weight of the club than does the shaft. This is because shafts can range in weight from as light as 40 grams to as heavy as 130 grams. The driver head mounted on those shafts would weigh between 190 and 210 grams. So if you want to seriously lighten the total weight of the driver, you need to get a lighter shaft.

The lighter the total weight, the faster you can swing the driver. And the lighter the shaft, the lighter the total weight, which means (I think you get my drift here) more distance.

The *flex* is the general, overall resistance of the shaft to bending. You know the flex by a letter—L for ladies, A for senior, R for regular, S for stiff, and X for extra-stiff. We designers know flex by a series of measurements of the *real* stiffness of the shaft, which we translate into a swing speed rating. Thus, a key element in matching the golfer to the shaft is to be able to measure the golfer's swing speed and only consider shafts that are designed with an overall flex that will match that speed within a narrow range.

What makes it tricky is that not all shafts of the same letter flex are designed to match the same swing speeds. You'd think it would be that way, but nope, each shaft maker is free to define its flexes however it likes. So the R flex from one company might be for a golfer with an 80 or 90 mph swing speed while the R flex from another is designed for a 90–100 mph golfer. And the same thing for all the other letters too! Interesting way to make the "tools" of an entire industry, right?

The *torque* of a shaft, or rather the shaft's resistance to twisting, is not such a big deal in shaft selection anymore. As long as you keep seniors, ladies, and men with a slow swing speed away from shafts with less than 3.5 degrees of torque, and big, strong, fast swingers away from shafts with more than 4.5 degrees of torque, everyone's going to be happy. Trust me. There are PGA Tour players using driver shafts with 4 degrees of torque and not suffering. So just follow that simple advice and you won't ever get torqued off about your torque.

Bend profile is the way the flex of each shaft is distributed over its entire length. Within most of the letter flexes you can have shafts that are stiffer in the butt end than the tip end, stiffer in the tip end than the butt end, and just about any variation in between. Why is that important? By changing the stiffness distribution over the length of the shaft, shafts can be offered to golfers that bend differently in different parts of the shaft to help hit the ball higher or lower within the same letter flex of overall stiffness. Or, by varying the bend profile, the shaft can send a different feel to the golfer using it.

Well, at least flex is something I am familiar with. I know I play a stiff shaft in my driver; it says so right on it.

No, you don't.

"No, I don't," what?

No, you don't know that you are playing a stiff shaft. The "S" you see on your shaft is completely meaningless.

We just touched on this above. Most golfers know, or think they know, that shafts come in a variety of flexes: S for stiff, R for regular, A for amateur or senior, and L for ladies. What most golfers don't realize is that those letters are just about the only things upon which there is universal agreement.

You say you want a "stiff" shaft in your driver? Fine. Whose definition of "stiff" do you want to use? Because one shaft company's "stiff" is another company's "regular," which may even be another company's "senior flex." Worse, the flex rating of one line of shafts might be at hopeless variance with that of another line, within the same shaft company!

Some of us tried to make it more specific. Back in the mid-to-late 1990s, I was part of a committee convened to establish testing standards for shafts so things like flex, torque, and a couple of other things about shafts could all be measured and compared on a level playing field. For three years we on the committee talked, and talked and talked. We finally adjourned with no testing standards because some of the companies were just too stubborn to agree to change their ways of measuring and defining shafts to agree with one uniform method. So here we are in the mid-2000s, still trying to define shaft flex with a letter instead of some real measuring method that could really tell golfers *how much more stiff or flexible* this shaft is than that shaft.

Each company that makes shafts knows exactly how much more stiff or flexible each of its shafts is as compared with the others, but you don't. And you're the one that's supposed to choose the right flex for the driver with which you play. So you get letters to choose among, put there by companies that all make their own individual and different standards for what those letters mean. See what I mean about this being an interesting industry?

But I'm just getting started.

Is that "stiff" shaft going into an iron or a wood? Because iron "stiffs" are stiffer than wood "stiffs." And you've said nothing about whether you want that driver in a steel shaft whose "stiff" may be stiffer or more flexible than a "stiff" graphite shaft.

If it sounds as though the concept of shaft flex is mixed up to the point of being almost meaningless, you are exactly right. If you buy a driver because it has a stiff, regular, senior, or ladies flex shaft in it, you have *no idea* what you are getting—nor does anyone else. Wait a minute; let me retract that. There *is* someone who *does* know, and that is yet another reason to spend some time with a professional clubfitter who lives, eats, and breathes shaft design and technology. Not all of them do, so if you are looking for real shaft guidance, you'll have to dig and ask around to find the clubmakers who are total shaft nerds. They're out there, believe me, because they barrage me with questions all the time to keep pushing their shaft-fitting knowledge deeper and deeper.

But flex obviously exists. I mean, some shafts *are* stiffer than others, aren't they?

Yes, indeed. But to determine that flex you have to toss out whatever is written on your shaft and move to more empirical testing. And even that has its problems.

In the past, most flex testing was done using one of two methods, called deflection or frequency testing. Deflection testing is based on a simple principle. One end of a shaft is anchored in place, and a weight is attached to the other end. You then measure how far the shaft bends, and that gives you the flex. Sounds simple, doesn't it?

But how much weight do you put on the tip end, and how much of the butt end do you clamp? Do you measure the shaft in its raw, uncut form, when it's cut to length, or when it's in an assembled driver? And exactly how much deflection difference constitutes a "stiff" versus a "regular"? All of these factors make a difference, and there is no agreement among the companies that make shafts on any of them. I told you some of us in this business tried to get all the companies to agree on how to test and report things like this but failed in the face of proprietary selfishness.

The other way of measuring flex is done by measuring the shaft's rate of oscillation or "frequency." In this approach, we start getting a bit more high tech. While the butt end of the shaft is anchored in a special electronic machine, a weight attached to the tip end is then plucked so that the whole shaft oscillates up and down. The machine counts the up-and-down oscillations over a fixed period of time and delivers a frequency measurement—255 cpm (cycles per minute), or whatever. The higher the frequency is (i.e., the faster the shaft oscillates), the stiffer the shaft will be.

So then, it's finally settled. We can know the true flex of a shaft by frequency testing it.

Um ... well ... not really.

I, along with a lot of custom clubmakers who are really into shaft testing and analysis, have been doing research into another performance factor that's at work in shafts, namely the distribution of the flex over the entire length of the shaft. Again, this is called the *bend profile* or *flex profile.*

Take three shafts each of which test out at around, say, 240 cpm—a nice red-blooded, all-American, R flex as defined in the testing labs of at least a few (but not all) shaft companies. Let's say that one shaft is stiffer at the tip section than it is in the center section, the other is stiffer in the center than it is in the tip, and the third is stiffer at the butt section end than either the tip or the center. All three clubs have a 240 cpm reading on the frequency analyzer, but all three will have very different playing characteristics.

In 2006 we finished the project and provided custom clubmakers with the means to determine the actual stiffness over the entire length of hundreds and hundreds of different shafts. See what I mean about the shaft nerds wanting to push their awareness of shaft-fitting deeper? Custom clubmakers who are using the TWGT Shaft Bend Profile System software can now provide a very specific answer to your questions about how one shaft compares to another one. The problem is that almost none of the information we just talked about is available to you when you buy a driver off the rack; yet it's all critically important.

What about the kick point, or I guess some people call it the flex point, of the shaft? I want to get some extra whip on the driver head as it comes through so I can get a higher trajectory and more distance.

Geeze, it's hard to know where to start with that question because there are so many mistaken beliefs intertwined.

All right, let's start with the notion of there being a "flex" or "kick" point. To begin with, there is no single point at which the flex occurs. Yes, you can bend the shaft and note a location where it starts to bend a little more, but the actual flexing of the shaft in motion is something that occurs on a continuum. There is no one place, like a hinge, where you can say the "flex occurs here."

Calling it a "kick point" is no improvement, because there is no "kick."

A lot of golfers think the shaft flexes back and forth like a fishing rod to catapult the ball down the fairway. Sometimes they call this "loading and unloading the shaft," but that's really misleading because it makes you think that the shaft flexes and un-flexes in the same plane, like a buggy whip. It does not.

The bending that occurs when you start the downswing does not flex back (or kick back) in the same plane when you hit the ball because we rotate the driver itself as we swing the club around our bodies when we make a full swing. This means the shaft bends back in a different plane than the one in which it bends forward, so it can't pick up bending speed from its initial flexing. A buggy whip and a fishing rod can do that because they bend forward in the same plane in which they were taken back.

Also, we golfers hold onto the club and shaft with our hands, which are very supple and fleshy entities. When the shaft starts to unbend from its initial bending at the beginning of the downswing, our hands don't allow it to keep whipping forward like a spring— our flesh dampens the bending action.

And finally, there is your notion that all this has something to do with the trajectory of the ball. In this you are partially right.

By far, the number-one determinant of the height of your drives is the loft that is built into your driver head. Okay? Let's keep that straight. But the shaft *can* contribute a little bit to that trajectory in this sense:

As you swing the driver back down to the ball, you have a wrist-cock angle. (You know, the wrist-cock is the angle between the shaft and the arms, and it has to "unhinge" and straighten out at some point before hitting the ball.) This unhinging of the wrist-cock is called the "release." The release of the wrist-cock applies centrifugal force to the driver head. The release also causes your arms to slow down in relation to the acceleration of the clubhead. That centrifugal force, combined with the slowing of your arms, causes the head to push on the shaft and *bend the shaft forward.* This causes the head to start traveling *ahead* of the shaft, in effect increasing the loft over what is really designed into the head when the clubhead hits the ball.

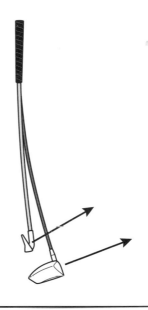

After the wrist-cock angle is unhinged, the shaft begins to bend forward. How much the shaft bends forward before the club hits the ball combines with the loft of the clubhead to determine the shaft's effect on the height of the shot.

As a result, you will find a number of shaft models on the market these days that are designed to offer a choice of low, medium, or high trajectory for the shot. Shafts designed to have a higher flight pattern will be more flexible, usually in the bottom or tip half of the shaft so that the forward bending of the shaft can be greater and thus increase the loft of the driver at the moment of impact with the ball. Conversely, shafts designed to hit the ball lower will be made so the bottom half of the shaft is stiffer. That reduces the amount of forward bending of the shaft and keeps the loft from increasing very much when the driver head meets the ball. In simple terms, that difference in how the stiffness is distributed over the length of the shaft is called the *bend profile of the shaft.* And that term has forever replaced the old terms of flex point and kick point. Got it?

So instead of talking about shafts as having a high or low bend point, we talk about them as having different variations of a bend profile. For example, a shaft can be made so that it is firm, medium, or flexible within the butt, center, and tip sections of each shaft's main flex. Let me give you a couple of examples of this from among the nine different bend profile options. A shaft that a PGA Tour player might prefer would be a butt firm, center firm, and tip firm bend profile. An average golfer with a decent swing but an earlier release of the wrist-cock on the downswing might better fit into a butt medium, center medium, tip flexible bend profile.

Well, shoot, how the heck am I supposed to know what bend profile I should be playing amidst all that gobbledy-gook?

Bear with me here, because I think I can express this without making it sound like you have to have the IQ of Einstein to understand it. I'll tell you how a good custom clubmaker would fit you for the right shaft.

The clubmaker first looks at your swing and asks you about your strength, swing athletic ability, and swing tempo, and consults with you to determine what shaft weight you need for the woods and the irons. Then comes a measurement of your swing speed with the driver or 3-wood and with a 5- or 6-iron. You need a separate swing speed with the woods to be fit into the right wood shaft, and the same with the iron shaft that's best for you.

All shafts in each of their individual L, A, R, S, and X flex models are rated by people like me and the shaft companies themselves for a swing speed rating. The clubmakers have all these data, so they can look at your swing speeds and know which shafts match. That's the starting point for the flex recommendation.

Then the clubmaker watches you hit balls and observes three critical things in your swing: your backswing-to-downswing transition move, your downswing tempo, and the point in the downswing where you unhinge the wrist-cock. If you have a very forceful start to your downswing (transition), the clubmaker will be thinking of shafts within your weight and swing speed range which are more firm in the butt section in their bend profile. On the other hand, if you start the downswing very passively, with a very slow buildup of the speed of the club, the clubmaker will be looking for shafts in the right weight and swing speed which are butt-flexible in the bend profile.

If you have an early release of the wrist-cock, he or she will be hunting for the shafts, within the right weight and swing speed ranges, that are more flexible in the tip section. A late release of the wrist-cock points us toward shafts that are tip-firm. Same thing is done with your overall downswing tempo for the center section of the shaft to note if it needs to be center-firm, -medium, or -flexible.

When the clubmaker is done, he or she then has a definite analytical reason to fit you into a specific shaft of a certain weight, swing speed rating for the flex, and bend profile description for the distribution of the stiffness within the shaft. The maker then consults tables and software programs that show what shafts have the right weight, swing speed ratings, and bend profile makeup to match your characteristics and makes a decision about the actual brand, name, and flex of the shafts for your clubs. Simple.

Yeah, right, simple! Can't I get this same shaft-fitting experience in a retail golf store or a pro shop?

Hit or miss. Or let me say the chances of finding a retail sales-person or club pro in a pro shop who knows all this and has the experience to take this approach is about one out of every one hundred, if that. People in golf-equipment businesses that know this stuff are pretty much total gearheads. To master the subject, you have to be to really interested in this level of detail about shafts, and that pretty much limits you to the most serious of the independent custom clubmakers.

But be aware that not even all clubmakers are into this deep enough to do this kind of analysis. Probably one out of every three clubmakers can do it. The best way to find a clubmaker with this experience in shaft fitting is to head to the web site of the Professional Clubmakers Society and refer to their list of "Class A Accredited" clubmakers. You find one of those in your area, and you'll find that you are in very good hands for your shaft selection.

As I go through this process, should I be looking for a steel or a graphite shaft for my driver?

That is a *very* good question, as there are advantages and disadvantages to each.

Remember what I said about the weight of the shaft controlling the total weight of the club, and the total weight being a big deal when it comes to how fast you can swing the club? The main advantage to a graphite shaft is that the vast majority of them are lighter than a steel shaft. Most graphite shafts for woods range in weight between 55 and 85 grams, with the vast majority being in the 65-to-75-gram range. Most steel shafts are in the area of 110 grams to 125 grams, although there are a number of new steel shafts which are being made as light as 85 or 90 grams. A lighter shaft means a lighter overall weight to the driver. A lighter driver means you can swing it faster and thus get more distance.

But steel shafts and graphite shafts send a different feel to the golfer when you hit shots. Steel shafts in general will feel crisper when you hit shots because the vibration you feel is greater. Graphite shafts, on the other hand, feel softer or more "dampened" because graphite as a material dissipates the vibration from the impact of the clubhead upon the ball. And when I say softer I do not mean less stiff. Graphite shafts can be any flex, from very limber to telephone-pole stiff, the same as steel shafts.

As I mentioned, graphite shafts are chosen first and foremost when you want a lighter total weight so you can maximize your swing speed. Another reason would be if your current steel-shaft clubs are starting to feel heavy and a little cumbersome to swing late in the round, or when you get to the bottom half of a bucket of balls. Graphite shafts are also good for golfers who experience joint pain from hitting the ball, because the graphite dampens most of the vibrations from impact so there is less aggravation of those sore hands, wrists, elbows, or shoulders.

Players who prefer steel shafts are usually golfers who are physically stronger, with a more forceful downswing transition and/or quicker swing tempo. The heavier total weight that comes from the heavier steel shafts is a good match to help such golfers keep from getting too quick or too forceful with the club during the downswing, to better keep the club under control. And of course, steel-shaft players should not have any preexisting joint problems, because the impact vibration level of a steel shaft is going to be harsher than with a graphite shaft.

What is "torque" in a shaft, and how does that affect my game?

Take a look at your golf clubs. Notice how the shafts all enter the clubhead at the heel? That means almost all of the weight of the head is hanging out away from the shaft. When you swing the driver down to hit the golf ball, all that weight sticking out there in front of the shaft wants to twist the shaft. The extent to which the shaft will resist those twisting forces is called (in the world of clubmaking, anyway) "torque."

When graphite shafts were first introduced, torque was a terrible problem; in fact, it almost caused the complete demise of the product. Since then shaft engineers have found ways of making graphite shafts so that torque is greatly reduced. But notice I said "reduced" and not "eliminated." You do not want to have a shaft that has zero torque because it would feel as stiff as that telephone pole I was talking about earlier.

With graphite, shaft designers can make shafts which have very low torque all the way up to a higher torque. Steel, on the other hand, does not have this design option. It will torque, but not enough to write home about. Steel in a tubular form has a built-in resistance to twisting, so the range in torque among steel shafts is very small.

So, how do I know which is right for me?

In some ways the decision might have already been made for you. Go into a golf store and try to find a driver with a steel shaft in it. The equipment companies have apparently already decided that you don't swing your driver fast enough. Right. Never mind that the average golfer shoots a 97. Never mind that the least of his problems is that he swings too *slowly*. Let them eat graphite. (What, you say the profit margin is higher on graphite shafts? Why, I am shocked!)

If you go to a custom clubmaker, however, nothing is fixed or built ahead of time. So here are some rules of thumb to help you decide between a steel or graphite shaft.

Use a steel shaft if:

- You are well above average in physical strength, and you prefer a higher total weight in the driver to help prevent your already quick tempo from getting any quicker.
- You have already tried graphite and felt the total weight of the driver was just too light to allow you to properly control your tempo, timing, and rhythm.

- You have tried graphite, and you simply prefer the different feel at impact that steel delivers.

Use a graphite shaft if:

- You really want to maximize your potential for more distance; a lighter shaft will allow you to achieve your highest swing speed.
- You are slightly above average to below average in physical strength.
- You have noted a recent loss in strength and body flexibility.
- You have lost distance with your clubs.
- You notice your clubs feeling heavier and requiring more effort to swing on the back nine or after hitting 20 or 30 balls on the driving range.
- You experience minor hand, elbow, or shoulder discomfort from clubhead impact with the ball.

Finally, IF you are going to use a graphite shaft:

- If you are a golfer with a quick tempo and a fast, aggressive swing, stay away from graphite shafts with 4 degrees or higher torque, and do not think shafts with a torque measurement of 3.5 or 4.0 degrees will cause errant shots. They won't. There are tour players who use graphite shafts with 4 to 4.5 degrees torque and hit the ball very well, thank you very much. But if you are *very forceful* with your downswing move at the ball, then OK, you can look at shafts that have a torque in the range of 2 to 3 degrees.
- If you are a golfer with a driver swing speed of 85 mph or less with average-to-smooth tempo and no real sense of aggression in the downswing, stay away from shafts designed with a torque measurement of 3.5 degrees or lower!
- If you decide to change shafts in your existing clubheads, be sure, be sure, and be sure one more time that the clubmaker will check and make sure the swingweight of the clubs is matched to the lightness of the new shafts.

And what about flex?

Okay, pull up a chair and get comfortable, because there's a lot you need to know about shaft flex before you head out to the local golf retail store or pro shop. And once you listen to this, you may actually discover why the vast majority of retail golf stores and pro shops are not the best place to head for a good shaft selection for your game.

Here's the deal with the shafts that are installed in the big brand-name clubs you see presented nicely in all those pretty display racks. The big companies know that it's a real pain in the inventory to offer their clubs to retailers with a variety of different shaft models with different weights, different bend profiles, and then different flexes on top of that. Besides, even if they did, the retailers don't want to have to stock all that many different options.

I mean, think about it. If you are a retailer and you have 20-plus golf companies wanting you to stock their drivers, you already know you need to stock some drivers with 9, 10, or 11 degrees of loft, and then each one of those lofts in a couple of different flexes. Do the math and you'll see why golf companies can only offer their standard-made drivers in one model of shaft with one weight, one torque, one bend profile without creating an inventory nightmare.

Specifically, which shaft should *you* use? The only way to know that is to have your swing speed measured by someone who can also assess where in the downswing you apply more (or less) bending force to the shaft, and can apply the other shaft selection factors mentioned here.

Whatever you do, do NOT buy a driver from any place that does not at least measure your swing speed and try to match a shaft to that datum. Without at least that information the person is simply guessing—and he's using your wallet to guess with.

So, what is a custom clubmaker going to do for me?

If that clubmaker is good, a lot … a *whole* lot.

A competent clubmaker will measure your swing speed, then observe your swing mechanics to look for things like your tempo, how smooth or forcefully you start the downswing, and where in the downswing you release your wrist-cock. He or she will then ask you some questions about how you want to see the ball fly and other performance factors to determine if what you want to achieve in the flight of the ball could be related to the shaft.

Next, the clubmaker will consult the files of shaft information obtained from suppliers, or from research on shaft testing that clubmakers have done and made available to each other. He or she will also have more precise lists of what swing speed matches well to what shaft flex for what shaft design. In other words, the clubmaker will have access to hard data on thousands of shafts and, whether it's steel or graphite, can pick one that is exactly right for you.

After that, the clubmaker will make a recommendation and possibly build a test driver for you to hit to obtain feedback. He or she may also have a launch monitor that can measure the launch angle contribution of the shaft as you swing the driver. In short, the clubmaker will come up with an extremely accurate recommendation of which shaft is likely to perform and feel best to you. In a retail store, when you buy standard clubs off-the-rack, you are buying a statistically average shaft that may or may not be well matched to your swing speed, swing tempo, how you start the downswing, and when you unhinge your wrist-cock.

I've read something recently about shaft spine alignment. Is that for real?

Some say there's something to it, some say there isn't. From my standpoint, it's one of those things where, hey, it can't hurt, so why not? What it boils down to is this:

There is almost no such thing as a perfectly round or perfectly straight shaft. If the shaft companies tried to achieve that level of perfection, you wouldn't want to pay the resulting price. You might not be able to see it with the naked eye, but most shafts are *very* slightly out of round, or *very* slightly crooked, or have slight variations along the length. "Spine alignment" or "spine matching" simply refers to finding how that imperfection affects the bending direction of the shaft, then finding a completely neutral position for the installation of the shaft in the clubhead so that that position points either directly at, or directly away from, the ball when the shaft is installed. The result is supposedly a shaft that is much more consistent in its bending characteristics as it carries the clubhead forward to strike the ball.

Now, everyone agrees that these little variations in shafts exist. What they don't agree on is whether it's a difference that makes a difference. You'll find golf equipment pundits who pooh-pooh the whole thing, claiming it's much ado about nothing. But you'll also find substantial test data that say there might be something to it.

I know for certain that if you have a really badly asymmetric shaft (yes, that *is* the term for a shaft beset with some of these little variations!) and realignment is not done, it would be very unlikely that the shaft would allow the clubhead to hit the ball straight and on center. I was deeply involved in the first real commercial testing of shaft alignment back in 1997, and I've seen the effects.

However, I don't want to leave you with the impression that you have a driver that is wobbling all over the place every time you hit a ball, because you might not. Things in the shaft manufacturing business have changed since spine aligning was invented, and unfortunately, again, there is good news and bad news in that regard.

Today, most of the higher-quality graphite shaft makers include a special test that is performed on every shaft to find a stable plane of bending before the shaft is painted and logoed. That's the good news. The bad news is that there's no way of knowing whether a company has performed this check on *your* shaft or not.

So, amid this vagueness there are two reasons for golfers to consider one of the various forms of shaft spine alignment checking.

- First, if you know that your driver is otherwise right for your swing (i.e., the right length, swingweight, etc.), and you feel that there are times that you make a really good swing at the ball but you hit it off center, this is a possible indication that your shaft is suffering from shaft asymmetry.
- Second, if you are a total golf equipment nut and you want to cover every possible base to be sure your clubs are exactly right, you might want to have your shaft spines checked.

If neither description applies to you, then don't worry about it. However, the next time you have a driver (or any club) made, you might want to tell the clubmaker that you would like the spine aligned. He or she won't mind (it's easy to do), and will be impressed at your consumer knowledge. And, like I said at the beginning—it can't hurt. It's an insurance policy against the shaft ever being the cause of poor shots.

What about grips? Is there anything I need to know there?

Glad you asked! If there is any part of the golf club that is most often overlooked, it is the grip. Most golfers initially select grips as an afterthought; we rarely, if ever, clean them, and most will wear them down until they look like something that would be used to rake cobwebs off the ceiling. Yet few things about the driver are more important, because the grip is the golfer's ONLY contact with the club.

Basically, the grip needs to allow you to control the driver without excessively tightening your hands. When you tighten your hands, you tighten your forearm muscles. When you tighten your forearm muscles, you develop "alligator arms," and your swing becomes short, quick, and cramped as opposed to long and fluid.

Having said that, I can only offer you one piece of advice with regard to the grip: *buy the grip that feels the best when you put it in your hand.* That's it.

We have all sorts of ways of measuring people's hands to get the right grip size. But what all those methods usually boil down to in the end is personal preference, and personal preference boils down to the way the grip feels when you swing the club. If you feel like you have to squeeze a little tighter to get the control you're comfortable with, the grip size or its texture are not right for you. A grip that fits well should make you feel like your hands *are* a part of the club, and you can use less grip pressure to keep control of the club during the swing.

Basically, you will be looking at two factors: texture and size.

With regard to *texture*, there are a number of general categories: smooth rubber, wrap-style rubber, full-cord rubber, half-cord rubber, urethane wrap-style, urethane smooth "panel" surface, and real leather wrap.

The *smooth rubber* grip has what the name implies: a smooth surface made of rubber, usually with little molded markings to enhance traction. A *wrap-style rubber* grip is a rubber grip molded to look and feel like the spiral wrap pattern of a leather grip. Thus, the hands and fingers will feel the grooves between the wrap surfaces.

A *full-cord* grip has little linen or cotton strings embedded lengthwise in the rubber over the full length and circumference of the grip to increase the friction level and help absorb hand perspiration. There are also *half-cord* grips, which are a cross between the all-rubber and all-cord grips. They usually feature rubber on the top half and cord on the bottom half.

The *urethane* grips are in essence an imitation of the old leather grips, but with the material of the grip made from a foam-backed urethane compound. Such grips may be wrapped or smooth "panel" in style and are usually characterized by their tackier surface feel.

With *leather*, you can now get grips that are leather-wrapped over a rubber underlisting. This makes for easy installation, plus you get the feel of leather. If you are really a purist, however, shaft-wrapped cowhide or calf leather grips are still available. However, they are rarely seen today, they are really expensive, and good luck on finding a clubmaker who is skilled in the wrapping technique. These clubmakers do exist and generally are recognized by the amount of gray in their hair (or the lack of hair to begin with).

Within each of those categories are a zillion degrees of surface hardness and types of texture design. Which you pick is completely up to you.

As far as *grip sizes* go, in general there are seven men's size categories each with a known (and agreed-upon in the golf industry, for once!) decimal diameter attached to it. These decimal diameters refer to the actual diameter of the grip at a point two inches down from the butt of the club. They range from 1/64-inch undersize, to standard, to 1/8-inch oversized. Any competent clubmaker can fit virtually any size grip out of any size shaft-grip combination.

As with texture, the only test that's important is the "fondle test." In other words, with apologies to the 1960s, if it feels good, play it. And one more thing: change your grips whenever they begin to lose that new, tacky, secure feel that made you choose the grip in the first place. In terms of feel, getting brand-new grips is almost like getting new clubs, and they really are not expensive to replace on a regular basis of once a year or every other year.

What's this thing called "swingweight"?

Okay, there are two ways to think about the weight of a driver. The first is the obvious one. You take the club, place it on a scale, and read how many ounces or grams it weighs. This is called the *total weight* of the driver.

The second is called *swingweight*. This refers to the *perceived* heaviness of the head of the club when you swing it. The idea is to set up all the clubs in your bag (except the sand and lob wedges, and sometimes the pitching and gap wedges too) so they require the same amount of force to swing.

Swingweight is not really a "weight" at all. Technically it's a ratio comparing how much weight is in the front two-thirds of the club with how much is in the back one-third. It's really more like a way of expressing the club's balance (i.e., how the weight of the driver is distributed). Let me explain it this way.

At one end of the shaft is the clubhead, which weighs a certain amount. At the other end is the grip, which also weighs a certain amount. In between, the shaft itself weighs something. When you grip a driver and waggle it, the head end has a feeling of heaviness that stands out over and above the weight of the rest of the driver. That's easy to understand, since the head is the heaviest of the three parts of a club. But some drivers feel as if they are very heavy in the head end; others can feel lighter. The golf industry embraced the idea of swingweight to compare the differences in that feeling.

If the golfer finds the right swingweight in the whole set of clubs, he or she will be able to sense the presence and location of the clubhead, from the waggle through the backswing, and into contact with the ball. If the swingweight is too light, the player will tend to swing too fast (ouch, almost never a good thing). If it's too heavy, the swing will be too slow or slightly cumbersome to make. Either way, if the swingweight is well matched to your strength, swing tempo, rhythm, and athletic ability, you will make swings that are more consistent and hit the ball more on center.

So, how do you find the swingweight? Or are you just supposed to waggle some drivers?

Well, no.

Measuring swingweight is not subjective. Since the 1920s clubmakers have been using a special scale to measure it. The grip end of a club is secured against the end of the scale, where the club can "teeter-totter" up and down on a fulcrum that is 14 inches from the end of the grip. A weight can be moved back and forth along the beam of the scale until the club is balanced level.

The slide weight will point to a letter-number designation such as C-6, D-2, or E-4. That is the swingweight for that club.

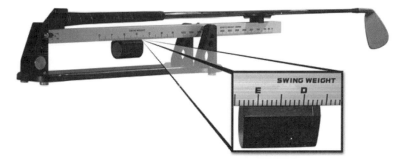

The swingweight scale used by almost every golf club company is designed with the fulcrum point 14 inches from the end of the grip of the club, and with swingweight designations in letter and number increments, i.e., C-9, D-0, D-1, etc.

The lower the letter-number combination, the lighter the head will feel when it is swung. The higher the letter-number reading, the heavier the head will feel. Most men's drivers coming from the factory are swingweighted from D-0 to D-2. Most women's drivers are built with a swingweight in the middle C range.

So, how do I know what swingweight is right for me?

Well, that's where things get a bit subjective. There is no specific way of determining what swingweight is correct for any golfer, at least not by direct measurement. Some golfers like a driver with a "heavy head" feel, others a light headweight feel, and many others have no idea what they like because they never have had the chance to experiment with different swingweights to find out.

That being said, generally, golfers of average to below-average strength, with slow, smooth, rhythmic swings (i.e., "swingers") tend to prefer drivers built to lower swingweights. Golfers with more upper-body strength, with rapid, forceful, aggressive, quick tempo swings (i.e., "hitters") tend to prefer drivers with a higher swingweight. *When in doubt, make the total weight of the driver light and the swingweight a little higher than what is average.* In practice what usually happens is that a clubmaker will ask if you have a club that just "feels right" to you. If so, it's probably because it has the right swingweight. Once the right swingweight is found, you should have all your clubs (again, except the sand and lob wedges) set to that swingweight.

While we're at it, I should also mention that there is another method on the horizon for matching clubs within a set. (I know, because we are pioneering it at Tom Wishon Golf Technology.) It's called moment of inertia (MOI) matching. Basically it involves identifying the club's resistance to being placed in motion. It requires the measurement of things like the driver's length, total weight, balance point, and pendulum period, and it requires a small computer to sort it all out, but you *will* be hearing a lot more about this approach in the future.

You've talked about everything but length. What length should I make my driver?

I've probably been procrastinating on that topic because it is a particularly sore point with me.

In my estimation, 90 percent of the men's drivers and 98 percent of the women's drivers sold in shops are too long for the players who buy them. If that's the case for you, then get your driver cut down and re-swingweighted to the shorter length, and don't be shy about doing it. Or go get a new driver fitted and built from scratch to the right length, and along with it, get the shaft, loft, grip, and swingweight that are best for your swing and how you play. Here's what's happening:

Let's start with the issue of distance. Most golfers believe that longer drivers will hit farther. They won't. Twice in my career I have conducted tests with real golfers and drivers of different lengths to see the effect of length on swing speed, distance, and ability to hit the ball on or off center. I can assure you that the only golfers who can swing longer drivers at a higher swing speed and still hit the ball on center are those who are: (1) low handicappers, (2) very good athletes with good hand/eye coordination, or (3) traits 1 and 2 together, along with having a smooth, rhythmic swing tempo. In other words, it's only a very small percentage of the golfing population. Every other golfer in the studies suffered from an increase in off-center hits with no swing speed increase at all as the driver length was increased.

But wait. The plot thickens.

There is another reason for having a shorter driver. It appears that, in the hands of real people, the shorter driver might very well hit the ball, not just with more accuracy, but farther as well.

Do you remember our discussion in chapter 1? For every half-inch by which you miss the sweet spot on your driver, you lose about five yards in distance. Miss it by an inch, and you lose ten yards.

Conversely, if you can gain enough control of the head to hit the ball even a half-inch closer to the sweet spot, you'll gain back almost all the yardage you think you're losing by using a shorter shaft. This, by the way, is the reason most people end up hitting shorter drivers farther. They're simply hitting closer to the sweet spot more often because the shorter driver is easier for them to control.

So, how do I find out what's the proper length for me?

Most people assume that if they are over six feet two or shorter than five feet eight, they need "inch-over" or "inch-under" length driver. Nothing could be further from the truth.

The length of your driver is not determined by your height; it is determined by the length of your arms in relation to your height, and then massaged from there to the final length by your swing plane and ball-striking ability.

The way a clubmaker determines proper length is by first measuring the distance from your wrist to the floor and locating that dimension on a chart that will give an initial driver length recommendation. But that is just the beginning.

Remember, the Holy Grail in fitting a driver is to get you the longest club you can swing *with control*. So, let's say your wrist-to-floor measurement says you should be using a 43.5-inch driver. Okay, that's fine if, and only if, you can control a 43.5-inch club! So the second step will be to give you a driver of that length and have you hit some balls—maybe with some marking tape on the club face. By watching your swing and seeing the results, he or she might be able to make your club a little longer or a little shorter.

Wrist-to-Floor Measurement for Initial Club Lengths (inches)

Wrist-to-Floor	Driver Length	5-Iron Length
27 to 29	42	36 1/2
29+ to 32	42 1/2	37
32+ to 34	43	37 1/2
34+ to 36	43 1/2	38
36+ to 37	44	38 1/4
37+ to 38	44 1/4	38 1/2
38+ to 39	44 1/2	38 3/4
39+ to 40	44 3/4	39
40+ to 41	45	39 1/4
41+ to 42	45 1/2	39 ½
over 42	46 and up	39 3/4 and up

In other words, your clubmaker will tinker until satisfied that the correct length for you has been found.

By and large, the only way most of the clubmakers are going to agree to make the driver longer than what your wrist-to-floor measurement suggests is if you, (1) are above average in your swing athletic ability, (2) have a normal-to-flatter swing plane, and (3) have good tempo and rhythm in your swing. If you swing "over the top," "outside/in," or slice the ball, staying right where the wrist-to-floor measurement says is as long as you'd want to go. In fact, some golfers who are less athletic, over-the-top, outside-in, quick in the tempo department, and not very athletic might be advised to go a little shorter yet. *Remember, distance is more about solid contact than anything else.*

Notice that these are all decisions best made by an experienced custom club fitter—not by the marketing department at some club factory a thousand miles away that has to make things standard so their retailers won't think they make too many options to stock in their store.

Okay, I've learned about driver heads; and I've learned about shafts. So, put it together for me. Exactly what happens when I complete my search for that perfect driver?

Fair enough. But when I get done with my description you might find it hard to believe that you ever hit the ball at all.

Let's say you're standing at the first tee. It's a beautiful early summer day. The fairway opens up in front of you like a luscious green ribbon, challenging you to hit the ball. The sky is a rich blue with wisps of white cloud high overhead. To your left is water, but it's not really in play. It just sort of adds an accent to the scene before you.

Your buddies have all gotten in their last-minute wisecracks about the quality of your game, and you step over the ball. You waggle once, twice. Then suddenly everything ... goes ... into ... slow ... motion.

As you start your takeaway, the clubhead does not immediately start to move backward, for its total mass (weight) is at rest and resists being put into motion. This resistance causes the shaft to bend or flex very slightly, with the result that the head lags behind the shaft minutely as you take it away. The head remains in a following or extremely slight lagging position through the remainder of the backswing, but you don't notice it.

When you get to the top of the backswing, the clubhead does not reverse its direction right away when you begin the downswing. Again there is a lag, just the right amount to let you know you are timing your downswing just right. The clubhead mass resists the start of the downswing, causing the shaft to flex. But because you had to rotate your body, arms, and hands around to get the club to the top of the backswing, this initial bending of the shaft happens in a direction that is up and down, not back and forth toward or away from the target.

As long as you keep your wrists hinged as you make the downswing, the club and your arms are accelerating at the same rate and traveling at the same increasing speed. But once you start to unhinge the wrist-cock, your arms begin to slow down and the club begins to increase its acceleration. Physics makes that happen; your arms are transferring energy to the club once you start to unhinge the wrist-cock on the downswing. But again, with the perfect driver you don't notice this. It just happens as natural as can be.

You remember seeing a trick-shot artist once at a golf show. He had put a clubhead at one end of a garden hose, and a grip at the other, and would hit balls. You remember being amazed at how he could possibly control that whippy contraption, yet here was your super-special, $400, high-tech, just-like-the-one-Tiger-uses driver doing essentially the same thing.

You look even more closely at the clubhead, and, to your horror, you notice two other things happening.

First, because the head is leading the shaft, the club face has closed. It is no longer pointed straight downrange, but is pointed to the left—a hook face. The more the shaft flexes, the more of a hook face it develops. At about one inch of flex, the head has turned inward about 2 degrees.

Second, as if that weren't bad enough, the shaft is also flexing in two different planes at the same time. As your eyes widen, you notice that the lie of the golf club has started to flatten out. Centrifugal force is causing the head to bend the shaft downward, with the result that the lie flattens about 1 or 2 degrees. At the same time, centrifugal force is causing the head to bend the shaft forward, raising the loft of the clubface 1 or 2 degrees higher than it was when you started the swing.

"You're dead," you say to yourself. There is no way you are going to hit this ball straight. In fact, you have no idea where it's going to go—but there is nothing you can do about it now. The elapsed time from the very top of the backswing to just before impact with the golf ball is about one-fifth of a second. The head has gone from zero to somewhere around 90 mph and, for all practical purposes, at this point you are simply along for the ride.

You can see the ball out of the corner of your eye and watch the head making its final approach. What surprises you next is that you never saw the exact point where the ball and the head made contact. It was too fast—much too fast. The total time from when the clubhead first contacts the ball until the ball leaves the club face is only about one-half of a millisecond (.0005 seconds).

What does catch your attention is the effect on the ball. The energy applied to the ball at impact approaches 4,000 pounds—two tons of force applied to about a three-quarter-inch diameter of that plastic surface of the ball—and causes the clubface to compress the golf ball 20 to 30 percent of its original diameter. But wait: the ball is not the only thing that is compressing and changing its shape. The face of your driver has been pushed inward about 1/16 of an inch from the collision with the ball.

After impact, the clubhead, reeling from the blow it sustained with that little 46-gram golf ball, slows to about 68 mph, and the ball leaves the club face at about 145 mph, spinning backward between 2,000 and 3,000 revolutions per minute. You don't know it yet, but the ball will remain airborne for 6.9 seconds and will land traveling at almost 50 mph.

After colliding with the ball, the golf club acts like a prize fighter who has just had his bell rung by an overhand left. The head is driven back, causing the shaft to flex in the opposite direction so that, once again, the clubhead is lagging behind the shaft instead of leading the shaft as it was when approaching impact.

The contact was a solid one, but you feel nothing through your hands or arms to indicate that yet. Finally, after the ball is about a foot from the club face and in flight, you feel it. You had always thought that you got a certain sensation of "feel" at the exact moment the club face strikes the ball. Not so. You do, in fact, feel the hit, but because of the time required for the impact to travel through the clubhead, up the shaft, and into your hands, and then to register with your brain, the golf ball is already 10 to 12 inches downrange. What you do feel, however, is a certain club heaviness, for the centrifugal force pulling on your hands at impact is the equivalent of 40 to 60 pounds.

You thought you were finished being amazed. Thus far during the swing, you've seen the clubhead alternately lagging behind and leading the shaft as it flexed. More recently, the clubhead assumed a lagging position as a result of the impact with the ball, which slowed the head down enough to allow the shaft to catch up and flex in the opposite direction. Now, during the follow-through, up to the point where the clubhead reaches approximately waist high, you see something that is almost comical.

The only word you can think of to describe it is: BONG! From the point of impact to the waist-high position, the clubhead alternately runs ahead of, then lags behind the shaft as it flexes. This occurs at least three times—as if it were a ringing bell.

Finally, an old familiar feeling runs up your hands and arms. It's what you've always described as the feel of the club, the thing you were always so picky about whenever you bought a new one. It was with a bit of chagrin that you now realize that this "feel" has little to do with club-ball impact and everything to do with the BONG—the flexing of head and shaft—that occurs long after the ball has left the club.

As you complete your follow-through, your head automatically raises to track the flight of the ball. As it does so, however, the world rapidly returns to real time, and you see your pure white ball pasted against the blue sky in a long arching dance with gravity.

You're not sure exactly what happened to you just now, but the drive was a perfect one—right down the middle, right where you wanted it to go.

Based on what you have just seen, part of you had concluded that it is a miracle that anyone, anywhere, ever makes contact with a golf ball. The other part of you is listening to one of your buddies giving you unfeigned congratulations for a beautiful shot. That's the voice you choose to listen to.

Shaken, but with studied casualness, you pick up your tee and say, "Oh, yeah, I hit 'em like that all the time now that I've found my perfect driver."

3 | Special Golfers: Women, Kids, Seniors, and Advanced Players

My wife is also a golfer, but does all this information really apply to her as well?

It does, but if you think it's difficult getting an appropriate driver off the rack for yourself, it is ten times as hard for your wife.

It pains me to say this, but, by and large, the ladies get a raw deal when it comes to golf equipment. Male golfers get to choose from among several different head designs from each company, driver lofts, and shaft flexes, in steel or graphite. Women get to choose from among one head model, maybe two but usually only one driver loft, and one flex of one model of shaft in one length.

If you applied the golf industry's approach to equipment selection to the clothing industry, here's what you would see in your local department store. You would walk through the men's department and see the usual array of sizes and styles from small to XXX-large, but when you get to the women's department, you would see clothing offered in only two or three styles and only in size medium. The same thing is true in the senior department. Customers would see only limited styles and one size to meet their clothing needs.

There are ladies, seniors, and even some junior golfers who can and should play with the same fitting specifications that you would find in men's clubs. And there are some men who can and should be playing with what are labeled by the golf industry as "senior," or "ladies" club specifications. In other words, good custom fitting is blind to gender and sees a golfer only as a person with a unique composition of size, strength, flexibility, and athletic ability in his or her swing characteristics.

Just because some company put a tasteful color on their golf clubheads does not mean that they are right for the vast majority of female golfers.

Are you saying those women's clubs are NOT appropriate for women?

In general and for the majority of women who are committed to playing the game, yes, that's exactly what I am saying. With various specifications on the clubs changed from the way they are on the standard-made ladies' clubs bought off the rack, the vast majority of women would play better and definitely enjoy the game more. But then, for the number of changes that would have to be made to most of the women's clubs displayed on the racks of retail golf shops, the player might as well seek out a competent clubmaker who can fit her and build that custom-fit set from scratch, with each specification tailored to her individual swing characteristics.

When you flip open a golf magazine or catalog and see an ad for women's golf clubs, the impression you get is that these are unique castings that are specifically designed for women. Sometimes this is true, but in many (if not most) cases, it simply is not so.

If you don't believe me, ask for or look up the design specs for a set of women's clubheads and compare them with a set of men's clubs. In most cases, the very key specifications that need to be modified for the typically slower-swinging woman are not modified—they are the same as they are on the men's model. And other things that are modified from the men's version are not changed enough, again not addressing the fact that the vast majority of women are not as strong, are not as athletically inclined, and have a much slower swing speed than the majority of men.

The majority of women's drivers which are a "ladies' version" of a men's model are only one inch shorter than the standard 45-inch and 45.5-inch lengths built for the men. And since you now know that the men who buy standard-made drivers off the rack are trying to play with a "number 1" that is longer than what the majority of PGA Tour players use, now you can see with a decrease of only one inch from the standard men's length, the ladies are in worse shape yet when it comes to trying to find a driver off the rack that really will work best for their abilities.

While the lofts on the ladies' drivers are higher than on the men's, they are not nearly enough higher. There are hardly any ladies' drivers offered with the lofts of 15, 16, 17 degrees that most average women golfers need to match with their swing speed for as much distance as they can muster from their swings.

And, just as with the men's clubs, you're going to tell me that the "L" in "L-flex" means nothing?

Actually, no. I was going to tell you that it *does* mean something. It means that the woman has no idea whether that one and only one shaft flex she is offered is too stiff, too flexible, or just right for her swing speed and swing technique.

See here's the unfortunate deal that women golfers put up with. In 30-plus years of fitting research, I have seen women who have driver swing speeds from 40 mph up to 90-plus mph. If I think about the average woman player at the average golf course, I see swing speeds from 50 to 80 mph. For proper shaft fitting, that should require three different stiffness designs of the shaft. Yet when women walk into a retail golf store, they see one letter—L— on the shafts, and they have no idea how stiff that L really is or whether it is an L that matches their 50-, 60-, 70-, or 80-mph swing speed. It's not that way with men who have A, R, S, and X flex shafts from which to choose to match their swing speed.

You remember that in the last chapter I cited a study that showed that shaft flex is not standardized, and, therefore, that its letter code designations for flex are virtually meaningless. That was true only for men's clubs. With the "L-flexes," the results of the study were both predictable and meaningful. Every one of the ladies' shafts tested was out of sequence compared to the other A, R, S, and X shaft flexes. Most were too stiff for a woman golfer with a 65 mph swing speed—especially when cut and installed to the final assembly length.

Given the importance of shaft stiffness in helping to get the ball up in the air and delivering a solid feeling of impact to the golfer, this is a serious problem. It means that most female golfers who buy ladies' lines of clubs may be having their game hindered by the shafts they are using.

Recently, a few shaft companies have come out with what they call an "LL-Flex." Translated, that means: "We finally figured out there are differences in lady golfers' swing speeds just like there are with men, so we decided to finally do what we do for men and offer you a choice." Thing is, these additional women's flex shafts are pretty much used only by custom clubmakers who buy shafts in component form and then identify which women need the more flexible or more stiff models. So that's one more reason that women really do need to consider seeing a good custom clubmaker to get the best match of clubs to their size, strength, and swing athletic ability. What's available in standard form, off the rack in the golf retail stores, just doesn't cover the gamut of what most women need to play their best.

Is there anything that IS appropriately designed for women?

Yes, the grips. It turns out there really is such a thing as a ladies' grip. Because the female hand is, generally, smaller than the male hand, the grip companies have all produced lighter, smaller-diameter grips for the ladies.

But, just because you are a woman, don't assume these grips are right for you. Remember the final test for a grip is how it feels in your hand. If you feel more comfortable with a larger "man's" grip, then by all means use it despite what any man might say—including me, as in the case of my triathlete wife who insists men's standard grips feel the best to her!

So, how then is a woman supposed to get a decent set of clubs?

Well, by now you know what I am going to say to that … get them custom built.

You see, a custom club maker does just the reverse of what a major club company does. The clubs you buy in the store are mass-produced to meet the needs of some kind of hypothetical "average" golfer. That's bad enough when it comes to men's clubs, but consider this. Last I heard from my "inside sources" in the golf industry, women golfers represent only about seven percent of golf club sales for the big golf club companies. Seven percent! How far out of their way do you think a major club company is going to go to cater to seven percent of the market? Now you know why women's club options are so limited compared to the men's.

For a custom clubmaker, national averages go out the window. These clubmakers operate on the principle of "one club, one customer, one clubmaker." It is drilled into the clubmakers' heads from day one that there is no such thing as gender or age when it comes to fitting golfers. There are only golfers with differences in size, strength, and athletic ability.

That makes all the difference in the world.

I see what you mean, but let's get back to the woman's driver. What advice can you give there?

All right, let's start with something I just said: "There is no such thing as gender or age when it comes to fitting golfers." In general, most women have a slower swing speed than men—around 55 to 70 mph. But some men have swing speeds in that range as well, so what I am about to say applies equally to both.

At that swing speed the biggest factors in choosing a driver involve getting the loft and the length right. So, use these rules of thumb:

- If your swing speed is 70 mph or lower, don't even think about using a standard driver unless the loft is 15 degrees or higher. And, even then, that's only if you generally do not struggle with getting the ball up in the air.
- If your swing speed is 70 mph or lower and you *do* struggle with getting the ball up, if your best shots fly no higher than the gutters on a one-story house, than even a 15-degree loft will not be enough. It should be closer to 18 degrees. If you can't find a driver head with that much loft, use a fairway wood with 16–18 degrees as your tee shot club. That might be a 5-wood by today's loft-to-head number averages, but because fairway wood lofts vary between companies, check it to be sure.
- If I am going to stand behind my belief that 90 percent of the men who buy a standard driver off the rack need to be fitted into a driver length that is shorter than that standard, I have to say that 98 percent of the women need to be fitted into a length that is shorter than what the companies make as their standard driver length. Generally 42 inches and rarely over 43 inches would be far more advisable for the majority of

average women golfers than the 44-to-44.5-inch lengths they encounter in most all of the drivers in any retail golf store.

And finally you should know that about the only place you have a prayer of finding a driver head with that kind of loft is by getting it from a professional custom clubmaker. Most of the big club companies do not make drivers for ladies with more than 13.5 degrees of loft. None I know of today has a driver loft higher than 15 degrees.

What about those oversized driver heads? Should a female golfer be using those?

There is no scientific reason why a woman golfer in the 55-to-70 mph swing speed range cannot hit a large titanium driver head, as long as the loft is high enough and the length is correct for the golfer. On the other hand, many women golfers simply do not like the look of a very large driver head. When it comes to clubheads, golfer psychology is not something to tinker with—forcing a head on to any golfer who is not comfortable with its size or appearance is a sure way to increase the number of poor swings.

So, ladies, if you don't like a big driver head, don't buy one. As you might already know—size isn't everything. There is nothing inherent in clubhead size that will make one driver perform better or worse, given your swing speed and ability to get the ball up.

What about that high-COR slingshot effect on the clubface? Does that apply here?

In a word: no. At these swing speeds, the high-COR "slingshot effect," or "spring effect," or "trampoline effect," or whatever you want to call the thing, will not kick in. The reason is that all the companies that make standard golf clubs have to make the faces withstand impact from golfers with the highest swing speeds. They don't want the bad image resulting from a caved-in driver face, so all their standard drivers are made so that they won't cave in until the golfer's swing speed hits 140 mph. Now, think about this. Higher ball speed comes when the golfer can flex the face to a greater degree with his or her swing speed. The higher the swing speed, the greater the face flexing force that is applied. So, if the face is made to survive 135 mph swing speed, how much do you think a golfer with a 55-to-70 mph swing speed will be able to flex the face inward and gain ball speed?

Now, in theory, this all could be addressed for average golfer swing speeds. There are no technological barriers to making a women's clubhead that would have that much spring effect built into the face. The problem is that the head could *only* be used by ladies (or men) with that swing speed, and no major company wants to invest that kind of money, and have the inventory problems of stocking them, for what amounts to about seven percent of the pie.

So, my point is that if the proper driver loft for your swing speed exists only in a smaller steel driver, so be it—don't hold out for a high-COR titanium head, because it won't make any real difference in distance for a swing speed of less than 80 mph.

Anything else a woman golfer should keep in mind when buying a driver?

Well, again, the two biggest things are more loft and a shorter length than what they'll see in 99 percent of the standard-made drivers stocked in the retail stores. But yup, there *is* one more thing. Why not consider an offset hosel?

Some, not many, but some drivers are designed with the hosel positioned more in front of the face, instead of the usual face in front of the hosel (see chapter 1). These "offset hosel" drivers are worth considering because moving the hosel forward helps to move the center of gravity farther back. This, in turn, helps the shaft increase the height of the shot. It also helps give the golfer just that much more time before impact to rotate the face closed, and thus helps reduce that tendency to slice or fade the ball too much.

What about kids? I am thinking of cutting down an old set for my son. That's all right, isn't it? I mean, he's only eleven.

Let me put it this way. If you want to make dead certain that your little Tiger or Annika will develop a swing as lame as yours, all you have to do is cut down a set of your clubs and give them to them. They will be too heavy, too stiff, the wrong loft, the wrong lie, and probably the wrong length. Other than that, they will be just what the kid needs to develop a great swing.

Should you perhaps cut one down just to find out if he or she will enjoy taking cuts at a golf ball? Sure, that makes sense, although you might first try to hunt for a single junior club for $5 to $10 at a used sports equipment store. As soon as you hear the young player ask for another bucket and complain about leaving the range too soon, that's the time to get them some proper junior clubs.

Since 2000, there have been a couple of companies who have made a real niche for themselves in offering good quality premade junior sets. Lofts are friendly, shafts are more flexible, weights are a little lighter, and grips are smaller. They offer the sets in categories of ages five to eight and ages nine to twelve, with the substantial difference being their lengths, designed on the basis of average heights for kids in these two age groups.

The only drawbacks to the premade junior sets may be their price and the possibility that your junior happens to be outside the national average for height for his or her age, from which the standard lengths of these sets are created. Thus we come back to your local professional clubmaker, who can custom build junior a set as well. And don't panic about that custom built part. It's been my experience that the vast majority of clubmakers do not charge prices for their junior clubs that come even close to the prices you would pay for the premade premium-branded junior sets found in retail golf shops. I've found that most custom clubmakers have a real soft spot for kids who are really getting interested in the game.

One last point.

Try to resist the temptation to buy clubs that are too long with the expectation that your children will "grow into them." They might well do that, but if the clubs are too long, you are forcing them to hit with something that could cause them to learn a bad swing, and you *know* how hard it is to UN-learn that swing later on.

If that means you need to get them a new set every year or two, get over it. As long as your kid is really into the game, it's a better deal than those tap-dancing lessons you sprang for, not to mention the $400 thin-profile/camera/text-messaging cell phone they just had to have (this month anyway). You're giving them a gift that will literally keep giving for the rest of their lives, long after you're gone. That's no small thing. Besides, it's a small price to pay for watching your son walk up the eighteenth fairway at Augusta with a 12-stroke lead, or your daughter take that dive into the pond at the Dinah Shore, right?

What about seniors? How much of this stuff applies to them?

All of it and more.

Let's start by defining what we mean by a senior. Are you talking about someone who has reached a certain age? That's not going to work, because I know some 60-year-olds who can move around like 30-year-olds. Are you talking about someone with gray hair and an AARP card in the wallet? Those criteria obviously don't mean anything.

I'd like to propose a more functional definition. I am defining a golfing senior as any golfer who has reached a point in life where he or she notices a loss of distance or loss of playing skills and attributes it to age. Note that this does not necessarily refer to a birthdate or the color of anyone's hair, but rather to a time in each golfer's life when the swing gets slower and the backswing gets shorter from a loss of body flexibility. That could be at age 75, but it could also occur at age 45. It depends on the person.

And THAT is the key ... *it depends on the person.*

To begin with, when the golf industry says "senior," they are talking senior men only. Have you ever seen an ad for a senior *ladies'* model? As if, somehow, senior ladies don't play golf? To the major club companies, however, you senior ladies are invisible because you don't make up very much of that small seven percent they pull in from the women's club business.

Second, most of the golf club companies do not really offer a specially designed senior model even for men. Other than the availability of an A-flex shaft, every other specification of the clubs offered to seniors is precisely the same as those of the regular men's clubs. That includes the absurd 45-inch driver, and very, very few driver loft options higher than 12 degrees. All these things are woefully inappropriate for what the golf industry considers the average senior man, I can assure you.

So, what's the difference between the designated "senior clubs" and the regular men's models? Basically, it's a logo on the head or shaft that says "senior," which has the dual function of (a) misidentifying the clubs as being somehow different and (b) offending most men over the age of 60.

On the other hand, look at what happens if you use a functional definition such as the one I just gave you.

If we define the average senior man as having a swing speed at or below 80–85 mph and at least some loss of body flexibility, then that man's needs are *very* different from those of the "flat-belly" players. The average senior needs more loft and a shorter length on the driver, shorter lengths on the fairway woods (which need to be offered at least up to a 9-wood), often a shaft more flexible than the typical A-flex, and no hint of an iron with a number lower than a 5 or even 6.

So, if the golf industry isn't going to meet our needs, what's a senior golfer supposed to do?

Let me start with a little heart-to-heart talk with you senior men.

I will not mince words here. What I am about to say can be confirmed by any professional clubmaker who's been in business for more than six months. By far, the number-one thing that gets in the way of a senior male golfer playing with the best equipment for his game is plain and simple EGO.

The problem is that Mother Nature has played a nasty trick on us. She has allowed us to grow into a 50-, 60-, or 70-year-old body. Okay, that's fine; we expected that. But what she didn't tell us was that the person inhabiting that body is the *same* person who used to run that flawless "sideline and go" pass pattern, or dunk a basketball, or hit 300-yard drives. In our heads, we still know *how* to do those things; but there is no way, nohow, that our bodies will ever again allow us to actually *do* them. *That* is the thing we have to come to terms with when we are choosing our golf equipment.

As a senior, if you are interested in playing the best golf you can play, then the game is all about common sense and playing as smart as you can play. I mean not only smarter than your opponents, but also smarter than the golf club companies as well.

So, how do I outsmart the golf club companies?

Simple. By choosing the kind of equipment you need, as opposed to the garden tools they're trying to sell you. This book is about drivers, so let's focus on that.

If your swing speed is still over 75 mph, don't worry; I'm not going to insist you retire the driver and start teeing off with rescue woods. But I will retire your *current* number 1 in favor of a new driver that has the following: more loft, shorter length, and a lighter graphite shaft that is also more flexible.

It might have a closed face angle or an offset hosel if you are developing a slice and/or for greater overall accuracy. I'll also make sure the grip is the most comfortable you have ever wrapped your hands around, and the swingweight/MOI of the whole driver will be rematched to your current strength and swing tempo.

And you know what? If your driver swing speed has moved down to 90 mph or less and your old driver has 10 degrees or less loft on the face, I will bet you dollars to doughnuts that this new driver with more loft will allow you not just to gain back the yards you have lost, but to hit the ball *farther* than you did before Mother Nature started to pick on you!

That sounds great but, I gotta tell you, the group I play with would needle me to death if I showed up with a double-digit loft and a senior or "L" flex on my driver shaft.

All right. You've heard the term "poetic justice," haven't you. Here's how you might dispense some of your own.

Press a little strip of lead tape over the loft number on the sole of your driver. You can say it's there to "adjust the swingweight" or some such. It'll stay there forever, and no one will know what driver loft you're using. Then, take a razor blade and just lightly scrape the flex letter off the shaft. It's only silk-screened paint or part of a decal, and it will come off with no damage to the shaft. Now, no one will know your new driver specifications and you can tell your buddies with the sharp needle whatever you want to about its details.

Then the fun begins.

Once they see you back up to the 150-yard marker, or at least farther down the fairway than you have been, they too will probably want a driver like yours. At this point you have a choice. You can either fess up with a Cheshire-cat grin on your face, or, if your relationship is really competitive with them, tell them it's a new X-flex shaft with a head that has 9 degrees of loft. Then start snickering when they rush off to buy what is for most people an inherently unhittable club.

And *that* would be poetic justice, if you ask me.

Tom, I hope you don't mind, but when I told the pro at my club I was coming to see you, he asked if he could come down and ask you some questions about his clubs. I see that he just pulled up.

Oh, hi, I know you! You're the head pro at Highlands Ranch just east of town. Welcome, make yourself comfortable, and let me know how I can help you. I know you're a darn good player because I read your name up near the top most of the time in some of the PGA Section tournaments.

Thanks. My questions center mostly around the shaft in the driver, because that IS the "engine of the club" for a player like me, right?

We-e-e-l-l-l, not exactly. But that's ok; I know just what you mean from my experience in fitting a few of the tour pros in my career. Most of the really good ball strikers in the game do tend to put a lot of emphasis on the shaft in their driver, because they can pretty much tell within one or two shots whether they like the shaft or not. You're interested in finding how to find that shaft in some manner other than trial and error. In other words, a shaft either feels right to you and you can pretty much do what you want with the driver, or it doesn't and you can't get the same results, am I right?

No question. But first of all I want to know what you mean when you say the shaft is not exactly the engine of the driver. That's what every one of my competitive colleagues believes too.

Part of the problem is that you guys who hit the ball well come up with your own conclusions for what you think the shaft is doing based on your experience, and especially on your sense of FEEL for the bending of the shaft and the FEEL of the impact of the ball on the face of the head. But just so I can help you the best I can, let me start this by asking you in your own words to tell me what YOU think the shaft does in the driver.

Fair enough. I know that when I hit a driver with the right shaft for me, it really feels like the shaft's bending is timed in such a way that it firmly "slingshots" the ball out there. If the shaft is too stiff for me, I don't get that feeling of the sling-shot action of the shaft, and the ball does not go as far. And if I get a shaft that is too flexible for me, it feels like the shaft shoots the ball up too high, and again, it goes nowhere. So I am trying to figure out how, when the new shafts come out that all the tour players flock to, I can determine if that shaft is going to be right for me or not, and whether any of the new shafts that come along are going to slingshot the ball farther for me.

Let me first start by telling you first what the shaft does NOT do in the driver, and why. Then I will tell you why you think it does some of the things that it doesn't, and then I will tell you how to deal with that. First, the shaft does not "load and unload" in a catapult or slingshot manner to hit the ball. It can't, and let me show you why.

Here, grip this driver as firmly as you can with your arms out in front of you so I can grab the head and do some bending with the shaft. I'm going to bend the shaft back, but I want you to keep your hands right there, firmly on the grip while I make that "load-ing bend" in the shaft. Once I get the shaft bent backward to simulate the loading of the shaft, then I am going to let go, and let's all watch what happens to the shaft and the clubhead.

Why, it just flexed back to a straight position and did not buggywhip forward!

That's right. Now let's take that driver over here, and I will se-cure the grip in the jaws of this bench vise. OK, we've got the grip dialed in between the jaws, and now I'll pull the head back to bend the shaft and let it go. See—here the shaft DOES act like a slingshot, whereas it didn't when you were holding on. The rea-son the shaft can't slingshot the ball is because your hands, and all golfers' hands for that matter, are not even close to being as rigid as the jaws of this vise. Your fleshy hands act as a shock absorber for the bending of the shaft to prevent the bending of the shaft back to spring forward. It can't happen.

So what does the shaft do for me when I swing the driver?

Well let's talk about that. First of all, the shaft is what chiefly determines the total weight of the driver. So you have to choose a shaft that will combine with the head weight and grip weight to make the total weight of the driver match as perfectly as possible to the physical strength you put into your driver swing. In other words, the harder you try to HIT the ball, or the more aggressively you go after the shot on your downswing, the heavier the shaft should be. But there has to be a proper balance between the total weight of the driver AND the amount of weight in the head so that you feel that the club is not too head-light or too head-heavy. And as a good player, I know you know the feel of too little or too much weight in the clubhead.

For sure. If the swingweight is too low, I really tend to get too quick, and if it's too high, I just feel like I have to put a stronger move on the ball with the club all the time. But you mention the total weight of the club in addition to the head weight feel that accounts for the swingweight feel. How does the total weight from the shaft weight combine with the swingweight, or rather how do I separate them out in my feel for the driver?

First of all, I don't want to infect you with a case of "paralysis due to overanalysis." One thing I know about good players is that you don't want to think too much about the driver during the swing! Grip it and rip it, as the *Daly Planet* says! So I'll explain this, and then when you get the right driver, you forget about it and just use that great swing you have. Let me ask you another question to get into this. Have you ever used a driver with a really light shaft, such as one that weighs no more than 60–65 grams?

Yes, I have, and the club just felt too light. It made me really struggle with my swing timing to keep from getting too quick with my tempo. I first thought it was more that the swingweight was too light. But when I put lead tape on the

head to increase the swingweight to get rid of the light feel, two things happened: the shaft felt like it was bending too much for my liking, and I still felt like I was fighting the tempo too much.

And you probably put a pretty aggressive move on the ball when you make the downswing, right?

Yes, I would say that I do try to HIT the driver. I always have gone after the driver a little more to get the distance I need to compete with some of these young bucks and their lightning swing speeds!

OK, here's the deal. You're strong, you have a strong move at the ball on the downswing, and you try to HIT the tee shot. That all puts you into the category to be better matched with a little heavier graphite shaft in the driver. You know, a lot of the shaft companies do make their high-performance, better-players' shafts in both a 65-gram and an 85- to 90-gram version for this very reason.

The good players who are more "swingers," or "rhythm players" as I call them, the ones who "ramp up" their downswing acceleration of the club to the ball, are able to use the 65-gram version of these shafts. But the HITTERS, the ones like you who are both strong and aggressive with the downswing, are better off with the heavier 75- to 90-gram graphite shafts in their drivers. This way the total weight is up there a little higher to help offset the tendency to get quick when the total weight is too light, and a swingweight increase doesn't do the trick to get that tempo back under a little more control. So that's the shaft weight issue in your driver that you need to watch. For everybody else, playing with the lightest shaft they can still control in their swing tempo is the right way to go with the big stick.

What else?

A good player like you will undoubtedly have a later release. I mean, you have the swing skill to hold the wrist-cock angle from the start of the downswing all the way to late in the downswing before you release the club and unhinge the wrists. That means

you definitely have the ability to see a difference in trajectory between shafts. Golfers who unhinge the wrist-cock too early in the
downswing, like a lot of the members at your club where you
teach, do not.

A late release generates the force to bend the shaft forward just
before impact. That does two things. First, the launch angle of the
shot is increased, depending on how stiff the shaft is in relation to
the force from your wrist-cock release, and second, this is where
you get feeling the shaft slingshots through the ball.

You mean the shaft is bent FORWARD when I hit the ball with my driver?

It's bent forward with ALL the full shots you hit with ALL the
clubs in your bag. Far less with the irons than with the driver and
the woods, but yes, for sure, with good players who have a late
release, the shaft is bent forward right before impact with the ball.
It is very rare for a player to be able to make the shaft actually lag
behind at impact.

Think of Tiger's "stinger" shot that he hits with a long iron or
one of his fairway woods. You know, the one that never gets higher
than the gutters on your house and just screams out there? To do
that, Tiger has to basically prevent the wrist-cock from fully unhinging until after impact. And in that rare case of a super-aggres-
sive downswing move with an incomplete release, the shaft could
lag a little behind at impact.

The amount the shaft is bent forward is limited, though. Even if
you hit a driver with an L-flex shaft, the shaft bends forward only so
far. Believe me, physics prevents it from flexing more as long as you
swing full through the ball. Sure, if you really steam your way down
to the ball but then immediately put on the brakes with your hands
and arms before impact, the shaft could bend forward a lot. But
that's a freak show event, since no one swings the club that way.

The more flexible the shaft, or the more flexible the tip half of
the shaft in relation to the grip half of the shaft, the higher you'll
hit the ball with your late release. So if you want to increase or
decrease the trajectory of your shots, you can switch around among
"high-" or "low-" trajectory design shafts and see a visible difference in the height of your shots. There are some good players
who do have more confidence in seeing the ball fly on a certain

trajectory than another, and the shaft is a way for players like you to customize that flight.

I've seen that in hitting clubs with different shafts, and I feel that difference in the bending of those higher- or lower-flight shafts too. Most often I feel that the higher-flight shafts feel more flexible than the lower-flight designs, but sometimes they don't, so that confuses me. I mean, it's logical that the more flexible-feeling shafts will hit the ball higher, right?

Without question, that's right. This is where an element of shaft design called the bend profile comes in. The shaft industry used to call this the bend point of the shaft. Bend point is a term that is dead and gone in shaft design these days because shaft designers now know what they were really trying to talk about was how the overall stiffness of the shaft was distributed over its length. So you can have an S-flex that is "tip flexible/butt firm" and you can have an S-flex that is "tip firm/butt flexible," which is just a generic term to let you know that there is a difference in how that S-flex stiffness is created over different parts of the shaft.

There are two reasons shaft companies do this, and two reasons good ball strikers need to know about this. For one, this is how the shaft can be designed to hit the ball on different trajectories. Tip-flexible designs will hit the ball higher than tip-firm designs for you guys with the late release of your wrist-cock angle. The other reason has to do with that thing that you and your fellow par-shooters have, and that we other golfers envy so much: this sense of FEEL that has to be right for you to like the total performance of a golf club. Tip-flexible shafts will feel more flexible through impact, while shafts with a tip-firm bend profile will feel stiffer and feel like they bend less through the ball. If you don't get the feel you want down there when you release the club to hit the ball, you won't like the clubs, right?

You got that right. The right bending feel for me in a shaft is really important. I mean, when the shaft feels right, I just feel like I can swing as hard as I want and still hit the ball solid. It just flows, if that makes any sense. When I hit a driver with a shaft that I feel is too stiff, it just feels more "dead," and I sense that I have to really swing harder to

make the shaft perform. And when I get a shaft that is too flexible for my tastes, I really get the sense that I am going to lose control of the club and the resulting shot. That make any sense to you?

Absolutely. One of the things that a custom clubmaker has to do in shaft-fitting for any good ball striker like you, pro or amateur, is to spend the time to find out what *you* like to feel from the bending of the shaft, both at the beginning of the downswing and right through impact with the ball. Most average golfers may know the feeling between a shaft that is about right and one that is much too stiff, but not all that many average golfers can detect a bending feel at the beginning of the downswing and through impact with the ball. Your expression of what you feel is then combined with an evaluation of how your swing affects the bending of the shaft, and both are then matched against the overall flex and bend profile of the shaft to come up with the right performance, and almost more important, the right feel of the shaft for you.

Isn't there any way to measure this? It sounds like a lot of judgment to me.

Well, we, meaning several of the "shaft-serious" custom clubmakers on this planet, have been working collectively to create a method of illustrating a graph of the bend profile of any shaft. With a graphed line for all shafts that describes their stiffness over their full lengths, we then can "lay one over the other" and see where along the length of the shaft and by how much one shaft's bend profile differs from the other. That way, we could take the bend profile graph of a shaft you like and compare it to the bend profile graph of any other shaft you may be thinking of using to see how similar or different they are in stiffness over their lengths. That way we could predict much more accurately whether you would like the feel of any shaft you may be curious about using in your driver, or any other clubs in your bag.

That sounds cool. And I can certainly see how that would take a lot of the guesswork out of shaft fitting. So where could golfers go to get this type of shaft fitting analysis?

Understand that this is all very new technology. Golfers would need to hunt down a custom clubmaker who has this new shaft bend profile software and book a fitting session. Right now, the best way to find a good custom clubmaker is to visit the web site of the Professional Clubmakers' Society at www.proclubmakers.org and look for the link for "Find a Clubmaker." When you can find a competent clubmaker in your area, give him or her a call and ask if they have the shaft bend profile software, or if they are competent in being able to fit shafts for players with a strong sense of bending feel for the shaft. Another place you can look is at www.twgolftech.com. Golfers can also look there for the "Clubmaker Locator" link and do the same thing with any of the clubmakers who they find are reasonably close to where they live.

So what else do better players need to look for in driver shaft selection?

Let me explain just how a shaft fitting should be conducted, how a good custom clubmaker will handle the task for ALL golfers, not just you guys who hit the ball so well that you make me green with envy! Just kidding.

First you'll warm up hitting balls while the clubmaker evaluates three swing movements in your downswing: the backswing-to-downswing transition force you use to start the club down, your downswing tempo/aggressiveness, and your point of wrist-cock release on the downswing. That's going to tell the clubmaker more about what shaft weight as well as what shaft bend profile design you would do best using.

Then your driver swing speed will be measured accurately. The clubmaker will then consult his or her reference materials to look for all shafts that have the weight you need which have a swing speed rating close to your actual driver swing speed. For example, let's say you have a driver swing speed that averages right at 105 mph. The clubmaker has seen your strong transition move, your more aggressive downswing tempo, and your late release of the wrist-cock, which tells him to look for graphite shafts in an 85- to 90-gram weight. He then will be sorting for shafts which are rated as 100 or 110 mph shafts which weigh 85 to 90 grams. Remember, there are so darn many shafts out there today that the clubmaker needs a process of elimination, so to speak, in order to get a manageable list of shafts to consider for you.

Next the clubmaker should ask you some questions to determine whether you are a golfer who depends on a specific bending feel in the shaft to be able to feel good about the shaft selection. If you are, which you definitely stated, he will ask you questions like: "At the very beginning of the downswing, do you like to feel the shaft bend noticeably, or slightly, or to give you a very firm feel, as if the shaft is not bending much at all?" And, "Do you like to feel like the shaft is 'kicking' through the ball, or like the shaft is really not bending much at all when the club moves through impact?"

The answer to the first question would tip off the clubmaker that you would be better off in an overall flex that is both a little stiffer than what your swing speed would indicate, as well as help the clubmaker select a bend profile design from among "butt-firm, medium, or butt-flexible." The second question would be aimed at determining if the shaft's bend profile design would best be "tip-firm, medium, or tip-flexible." He may also ask you to name some shafts that you have liked, as well as shafts you have felt to be too firm or too flexible. In short, it is all a process of elimination to come up with a small group of shafts that meet your swing speed, swing movements, and feel criteria. In other words, it will all require less trial and error.

The thing is ... this is exactly the same process a custom clubmaker would use for a 30, 20, 10, or scratch handicap player. The difference is that if the golfer can not express any specific feel requirements for the shaft, the clubmaker will do the selection based on what he sees in the golfer's swing speed, transition, tempo, and wrist-cock release.

So you're saying that the way a golfer starts the downswing, the golfer's downswing tempo, and when the golfer unhinges the wrist-cock on the downswing all combine to determine the final flex and the bend profile design of the shaft that is best?

You got it. And that's all because there are currently no standards for what constitutes an L, A, R, S, or X flex. If we know the swing speed rating for any given shaft, that is far better for pinpointing the shaft's overall stiffness than some undefined letter printed on it. For example, I can name you several A, R, and even S flex shafts in the game that all have the same swing speed rating! So, the first thing that better players—heck, I mean ALL players—have to know about shaft fitting is that they cannot possibly pick the right flex by referring to a letter printed on the side of the shaft. You have to be able to refer to a swing speed rating for any given shaft to know if its general overall stiffness is close to what you need or not. Please, forget about the letter. It really is meaningless.

How do you know what the swing speed rating is for the flex of any shaft?

Several sources provide this information. First, you can visit the web site of any of the better-known shaft makers such as True Temper, UST, Aldila, Fujikura, and so on, and find the swing speed rating for each model and flex of the shafts they make. Custom clubmakers also have swing speed ratings for all of the shafts they could order among those provided by their suppliers. Unfortunately, you won't find this type of information for the shafts that the brand-name clubmaking companies install on their standard, off-the-rack, retail clubs. They still go by the L, A, R, S, or X designations, and in all my years of experience in the golf equipment industry, I have not once seen a company that sells standard-made clubs bought off the rack in a retail golf store/pro shop ever create or provide this type of information for their retailers.

What do the golfer's swing characteristics mean when it comes to shaft fitting?

I mentioned there are three swing characteristics that play an important role in matching the golfer with the right shaft. The first of these is the backswing-to-downswing transition, how forcefully the golfer starts the club down to the ball.

In shaft fitting we see three basic variations of the transition. First, and not all that prevalent, is the *smooth transition*. This is the golfer who may actually have a distinct pause in between the end of the backswing and the beginning of the downswing, or who starts the downswing with a very gradual buildup of speed. That transition puts very little bending force on the shaft, so these golfers usually are better matched with shafts that have a swing speed rating that is a little lower, or a little more flexible than the golfer's swing speed. A smooth transition is also better matched to a bend profile design that has a more flexible butt section, or more flexible grip end of the shaft.

Examples of Swing Speed Ratings for Driver Shafts

Shaft Company	Shaft Name	Flex	Swing Speed Rating*
Aldila	NV-65	R	85–95 mph
Aldila	NV-65	S	95–105 mph
Aldila	NVS-65	R	80–90 mph
Aldila	NVS-65	S	90–100 mph
Fujikura	Tour Platform 26.3	R	80–90 mph
Fujikura	Tour Platform 26.3	S	90–100 mph
Fujikura	Vista Tour 70	R	90–100 mph
Fujikura	Vista Tour 70	S	100–110 mph
Grafalloy	Blue	R	90–100 mph
Grafalloy	Blue	S	100–110 mph
Grafalloy	Blue Superlite	R	80–90 mph
Grafalloy	Blue Superlite	S	90–100 mph
UST	ProForce 65	R	80–90 mph
UST	ProForce 65	S	90–100 mph
UST	Harmon Tour 60	R	75–85 mph
UST	Harmon Tour 60	S	85–95 mph
True Temper	Dynamic Gold Steel	R-300	85–95 mph
True Temper	Dynamic Gold Steel	S-300	95–105 mph
True Temper	Dynamic Gold Steel	X-100	105–115 mph
True Temper	TX-90 Steel	R	80–90 mph
True Temper	TX-90 Steel	S	90–100 mph

*Swing Speed Rating is for the golfer's driver or 3-wood swing speed.

The chart lists the swing-speed ratings for a sampling of shaft models of different letter flexes for drivers and fairway woods to show how the same letter flex designation can represent shafts that require a different swing speed from the golfer to be considered reasonably well fit to the overall stiffness design of the shaft.

Next is the *strong transition*. This is the golfer who can't wait to accelerate the club and get it up to full speed. This golfer really gives the sense of pulling hard on the club to start the downswing. In many cases, you can actually see the shaft bend with your own eyes when a strong transition is put on the club. These golfers are better fitted to shafts with a swing speed rating that is a little higher than the golfer's actual swing speed and a butt-firm bend profile design.

Finally, in between is the average transition. This comes from the golfer who gives the impression of starting the downswing

The downswing transition is a difficult swing move to see in still images. However, by focusing on the graphic enhancement in each photo, it is possible to convey the point of the start of the downswing being forceful, average, or smooth in the start of the acceleration of the club down to the ball.

with some force, but not with a really sudden increase in the speed. For these golfers, the clubmaker will choose shafts so that the golfer's swing speed is right in the middle of the shaft's swing speed rating.

The next swing move that has a bearing on shaft selection after the transition is the downswing tempo of the golfer. It is evaluated as being fast/quick, average, or smooth. Again, just by my telling you the variations in the downswing tempo, you can get a feel for what each of these three looks like in the swing. The fast/quick tempo is, of course, associated with the player who really ramps up the speed of the club to the ball during the whole downswing. This player is really giving you the sense that he or she is trying to clobber the ball. Opposite to that is the smooth-tempo player who gives the impression that the club is moving to the ball very passively, with only a hint of acceleration. And, finally, we have the "in-between" golfer with an average tempo, who seems to be trying to hit the ball with some force, but not nearly as much as the fast/quick tempo golfer.

Here, the faster the swing tempo on the downswing, the more the golfer should be matched to a shaft with a slightly higher swing speed rating than his or her own actual swing speed, as well as a butt-firm bend profile design in the shaft's distribution of stiffness. And the smoother the tempo, the more the golfer would be fitted into a shaft with a little lower swing speed rating and more butt-flexible bend profile design.

The unhinging of the wrist-cock on the downswing is called the release. In general terms (and from left to right in the photos), golfers can have an early, midway, or a late release of the wrist-cock angle during the downswing. Being able to identify each general type of release is important for fitting the best shaft tip section design for each golfer.

Finally, there is the matter of the point on the downswing at which the golfer unhinges his or her wrist-cock angle. This is a swing characteristic clubmakers use to identify whether the bend profile needs to be more tip-firm, tip-medium, or tip-flexible in its design. If the golfer unhinges the wrist-cock in the first half of the downswing, otherwise known as "casting off the club," that indicates a tip-flexible bend profile. Players with a late release would more likely be happy with a tip-firm bend profile design so the shaft won't kick the ball too high and won't feel too flexible through impact with the ball. That's pretty much the procedure and technique that good clubmakers use to fit golfers with the right shaft for their swing.

OK, so I got that part about the shaft pretty well down, at least in terms of how I ought to look for what I need. Since we've dwelt a bit on the shaft, what about the other specifi-

cations of the driver? As a reasonably good ball striker, what else do I need to know to make sure I get the best driver for my game?

Really, the answer to that question is no different for you than for the middle- and higher-handicap player. The four most influential specifications of the driver in order of how much effect they will have are: length, loft, face angle, and the swingweight or moment of inertia of the driver. You might well end up with a substantially different length, loft, face angle, and swingweight/MOI than the mid- and high-handicappers, for sure, but their contribution to performance is every bit as important for you better ball strikers to nail down for YOUR swing.

Here's a tricky statement for you. *When it comes to the length of your driver, you want to be playing with the longest length that you can control and hit on center the highest percentage of the time.* Now, you might think that statement is obvious, but think about it for a minute.

The trick is that if you focus on the second half of that statement, you are a smart golfer. If you heard the first part of the statement and fogged out on the second part, you'll end up with a driver that is too long to make the second part of the statement happen when you play! But here's why this is so important for you as a better player to focus on part two of that statement.

You are a good enough "golf athlete" that you probably will get a little higher swing speed with a longer driver. Good golf athletes can keep the club on plane and retain the proper moment of wrist-cock release when they pick up a little longer driver. Less-skilled golfers usually end up losing some swing speed or, at best, end up with the same swing speed when they play with a longer driver. The reason is that a club too long for their swing ability *will* break down their swing plane and wrist-cock angle. But if you do have the golf athletic ability to maintain a decent swing plane and release, should you be playing with a longer driver? No. Not unless you can hit the ball on center and solidly the same percentage of the time that you can with a little shorter driver.

And there's the kicker with many good players. They get fooled into thinking they are going to be giving up distance if they drop down to a little shorter driver length, so they keep trying to drive to the best of their ability with drivers that really are too long.

You better ball strikers should know above all others that consistency is the name of the game off the tee—consistently solid and consistently in play. Few players who hit the ball aggressively can achieve both with a 45-inch driver length. Period. If good players would realize that as long as they get the right loft, shaft, and swingweight/MOI in the driver for *their* swing, the difference in distance between a 44-inch and 45-inch driver is minimal.

Two things have happened on the PGA Tour in the last three years that have kept drive distances slightly increasing. The majority of the pros are playing a little more loft and a little less length on their drivers. Now, think about it. The average driving distance is still increasing slightly, but it's doing that as lofts are increasing and lengths decreasing.

Plain and simple, that means custom fitting is what is squeezing out more distance for these guys. So *any* good ball striking amateur, and I mean from plus whatever up to seven, who has grabbed the same driver model off the rack as is "being played on the tour," picked it with the tour players' loft, reshafted it with a "name" shaft that is popular on tour at the same length the club had off the rack, well, that is not the smartest way to go to really have a chance at improving your tee shot game.

As a better player, if you have the swing speed, transition, tempo, and release that the tour players have, use the same shaft models and flexes they use. But if you're *not quite there* with the same swing moves, then get fitted into the shaft that realistically matches your swing speed, transition, tempo, and release.

The same thing is true with the length and loft. If you don't have the swing speed and angle of attack the pros do, get the loft that is going to maximize *your* swing speed and angle of attack into the ball. And if you remember that despite the few guys out there who will experiment off and on with a longer driver length, the last I checked, the average driver length out on tour was 44.5 inches, which is one-half to one inch shorter than the length of most drivers sitting on the racks of the retail golf stores. In other words get smart and get fitted with clubs that bring out the best in *your* game. That's what the tour players do!

How about the practice of carrying two drivers in the bag, like Phil Mickelson did at this year's Masters Tournament? Is

that something that only advanced players should think about or not?

That was interesting to see two drivers in Philly Mick's bag this spring, wasn't it? To me, that is a perfect example of a player using his old noggin to play smart golf by tailoring a part of his or her equipment to address certain possible weaknesses in his or her game.

In Phil's case, he took advantage of the way that weight can be distributed to different areas in a driver to create an intentional fade or draw with the same swing. Even for the tour players, having to make that little change in their stance, swing, or hand position at impact to intentionally fade or draw the ball brings about a higher chance of making a mistake and seeing the shot fly where they don't want it to go.

In my opinion, having "one for fade and one for draw" is only something that a pretty darn good ball-striker is going to benefit from, depending on the design of the par-4 and par-5 holes which have a dogleg one way or the other. For the majority of players who are decent ball-strikers but not of tour quality, I think the two-driver approach might be better done by having one driver that is shorter in length to hit on tight tee shot holes, and one to let loose with on holes where there is little if any trouble off the tee. On the other hand, a two-driver approach is not the way to go if the club you have to leave out of the bag to keep your total at 14 is one that you might need.

For average to less-skilled players, the main focus has to be on being properly fitted for ONE driver that they can hit straighter and a little farther than their standard-made, off-the-rack, one-size-fits-all driver. Since there are so many golfers who have no idea what real custom fitting can bring to their party, that's the real goal they should be focused on before ever considering messing with two different drivers.

You mentioned drivers on which the weight can be moved around the head to influence the flight of the ball. Is that something that golfers should think about as a way to correct a misdirection problem with the ball?

NO, and that's stated as emphatically as I can utter it! For you as a good ball-striker and any other players like you who do not chronically slice or hook the ball, the drivers that allow you to move *enough weight* around the head are a good thing for "shutting down one side of the fairway," if you know what I mean.

Sure, you mean when you step up to the tee and you know that 99 times out of 100 you're going to hit the ball with a slight fade or draw only. That way you can aim more to one side of the hole and let that slight fade or draw have more fairway to land in.

Absolutely. And when you can do that with your driver, you effectively give yourself twice as much fairway width in which to land the tee shot. Note that I said the drivers that allow you to move *enough weight* around the head. The problem with most all of these weight-movement drivers is that they don't provide enough weight to really make a truly visible change to the flight of the ball for anyone but a really good ball-striker. Since I was the first club designer to create a metal wood with intentional weight movement, I know it takes well over 30 grams of movable weight before the majority of golfers could ever see the effect this kind of club has on the shape of their shots. Weight-movement drivers that allow you to move 20–25 grams around the head to change the shape of the shot are OK for really good ball-strikers, and that type of player will notice a 5- to 10-yard change in the directional flight of the ball.

But the average golfer whose ball flight is not all that consistent, even among their good shots, won't really get enough weight change to really make a truly visible change in the shape of the shot. What's worse are the golfers who slice or hook the ball 25 yards or more who think that moving the weight to either side of the driver head is going to cure their slice. That can't happen because for one thing, they would need to be able to move 40 grams around the head to really see the effect on their errant shot pattern. For another, players with this much of a slice or a hook are far better off using a face angle change or in the case of the slicers, moving into a driver with an offset hosel. Those fitting changes *will* result in a reduction of a slice or a hook of that magnitude. So in the end, because few if any of the weight-movement drivers allow you to move as much as 40 grams around the head, these models that have become available since 2004 are really only for the better ball-strikers to use to be able to be more consistent with their ball flight.

4 Seeking the Holy Grail

I know that throughout this book you've been saying we should all have our clubs custom built. That's fine but come on, that's only for really good players like my pro here, right?

Nope! The truth is exactly the reverse of that.

Look at it this way. People like your pro and low handicappers are skilled enough to be able to play well with almost *any* golf club. You, on the other hand are not, which means YOU need properly fitted golf clubs even more than THEY do. *You and every other golfer needs custom fitted clubs to minimize the swing errors you have and to maximize your swing strengths.*

Now, let's be clear—I am NOT saying you can buy skill as a golfer. I am not saying that by spending enough money, you can somehow go from being a double-digit handicapper to qualifying for next year's U.S. Open. Buying new clubs—even truly custom built ones is NOT a substitute for learning and "grooving" the proper swing fundamentals. Never has been. Never will be.

I AM saying, however, that equipment that doesn't fit—that is the wrong length, or loft, or weight, or balance—can keep you from being all that you could be as a golfer, regardless of your handicap.

You see, golf is inherently a difficult and often frustrating game, but that's part of its charm, part of the fun. As with any game, however, if poorly fit equipment makes it so you can't improve to whatever level your natural ability can take you, suddenly it becomes a whole lot less charming and not fun at all.

The problem, though, is that I know less about what to look for in a custom club fitting than I do about the clubs themselves.

Well, you're not alone. And adding to the confusion is that there are many definitions of what constitutes custom fit golf clubs or a custom fitting session. One of my colleagues in the clubmaking business perhaps described it best when he used the analogy of a car wash.

Let's say your car is looking pretty trashed out. At one level, you can hose your car down with water and squirt off the worst of the dirt. That's an improvement. Not great, but better than nothing. At the next level, you can get out the bucket and soap and give the car a good scrubbing. That's even more of an improvement. Or you can pull out all the stops and scrub it, rub it out, wax it, and detail it inside and out. Now you're ready for show time. The point here is that each of the above can be described as "getting the car washed."

Getting custom fitted for golf clubs is much the same. There are several levels, and all can (and have) been described as custom fitting. Since a lot of club companies and golf equipment retailers are becoming aware that custom fitting is about to become more "in," golfers are going to be seeing a lot of things that will be billed as custom fitting. That's why it's really important for golfers to know what is and is not a real custom fitting session. Let me give you a quick summary.

Level One (The UN-fitting): Believe it or not, there are some who feel that hitting a few shots with provided drivers at a driving range, during a trial-and-error "Demo Day," is an exercise in custom fitting. Wrong. While it sounds good to "try before you buy," Demo Days are in no way a custom fitting, because no effort is being made to try to customize the drivers being hit to the individual size, strength, and swing mechanics of the golfer.

Level Two (The "Is That All" Fitting): A number of golf companies have created neat fitting carts filled with clubs whose lot in life is to sit patiently on the driving range until someone comes over and pays attention to them. The vast majority of fitting carts are created to "fit" irons, but only in the company's one or maybe two iron models, which are shafted with one model of shaft, in a couple of different flexes.

The only specifications which are custom fitted are length, usually within a plus one-half-inch to minus-one-half-inch range from the company's standard, along with the lie angle, which, in the real world, can be fitted properly only by using a dynamic lie test board. What's missing from a real iron fitting are: (1) a wider selection of iron head models, (2) a wider selection of shaft weight, shaft bend profile, and flex, (3) a proper means of identifying the correct length for the golfer outside of the "here, try this" approach, (4) the proper swingweight or moment of inertia to match the golfer's strength, swing tempo, and athletic ability, and (5) the most comfortable grip model and size.

Oh, did we forget the woods in this cart fitting? Most golf company fitting carts do not address wood-fitting and are filled only with irons. However, those that do include woods also fall well short of offering the golfer the full complement of fitting specifications that you would find in a real custom fitting session. Which ones? How about: loft angle and face angle options to correct for misdirection problems, a wider variety of shafts in different weights, bend profiles and flexes, short enough lengths to meet the needs of the vast majority of golfers, a variety of swingweights, not to mention a variety of grip types and sizes?

Level Three (The I *Think* I Had A Custom Fitting Fitting): A lot of golfers would consider hitting shots on a launch monitor at a retail golf store as a higher level of fitting. And they'd be right as long as: (1) the operator of the launch monitor really knew how to translate the results into accurate fitting specifications, (2) the fitting session lasted at least 30 to 45 minutes and included several other measurements and analyses, and (3) the driver they fit you with required you to come back another day to pick it up, because alterations had to be done to it. If your fitting session lasted 15 minutes or less and/or if the driver into which you were "fitted" was selected from the store's off-the-rack inventory, you were not really custom fitted.

The other Level Three fitting that exists comes through the online questionnaires that some of the well-known standard clubmaking companies offer. Let me be frank about these services. They do a better job of getting you into a proper driver than 80 percent of the retail golf stores can. But again, because they can't see you swing, and because they fall short in the number of possible fitting options available to them, they fall well short of a Level Four fitting.

Level Four (Now *That* Was a Custom Fitting): When you enter the world of a Level Four custom fitting, you usually enter the shop of a trained and experienced custom clubmaker where the focus is on one club at a time, not 50 drivers a day sold off the rack. Think of it as golf's equivalent to a trip to a custom tailor shop.

Prepare to spend at least an hour, likely longer, with the clubmaker as everything from your current set, to your swing, to your manner of play and your priority for improvement are queried and analyzed. You'll have a choice of many different shapes, styles, and designs of clubheads from which to choose. The options for possible shafts and grips for your swing will number in the triple digits, not whatever was installed in the club to begin with.

In short, your custom set will be built from the ground up to meet all your playing and game improvement requirements, not altered from something sitting on the rack. You'll likely have to make at least two and probably three trips to the clubmaker's workshop, as details are massaged and tweaked into the final individually made product. And you'll be amazed that you won't pay any more than you would for a standard made off-the-rack club.

Level Five (The I Think I Died and Went to Heaven Custom Fitting): Theoretically there is a Level Five but, unless you are a PGA Tour pro, or the best friend of a golf company designer or CEO, you'll never see it. We're not just talking about custom fitting all 23 specifications to your individual playing needs. We're talking about the clubheads themselves being custom designed and produced *only for you*. In other words, you get a true "one of a kind, no other clubheads in the world are like this" set of custom fitted *and* custom made clubs.

It usually requires several visits, between which the clubmaker will be grinding, shaping, testing, and tweaking every performance aspect of the clubheads, shafts, grips, and the assembled specifications. The clubheads may be created with a different sole shape, toe profile, topline thickness, amount of offset, or a variety of other little things that will make them quite different from any other golf club on the planet.

And what about the clubmakers themselves? How do I know if he or she is any good?

During my career, I have taught nearly 200 clubmaking schools and over 2,500 different clubmakers. I developed the first clubmaker accreditation testing programs to verify the skills of clubmakers, and I have written six other books plus a handful of videotapes that served as instructional materials for teaching clubmakers the skills of the craft. In short, I have seen tons of clubmakers in my life and I know there are differences in what they offer and how they do their work.

First, I need to tell you that there are clubmakers who are experts in club fitting, and then there are clubmakers who are assemblers of golf clubs. There is a huge gap between the simple workbench skills needed to build a set of clubs and the knowledge necessary to fit a golfer with the *right* golf clubs.

The technique for properly attaching the clubhead and grip to the shaft can be taught in three hours and perfected in a day of practice. How to fit a golfer with the right specifications of the clubhead, shaft, grip, and assembly is something that takes years to master. In fact, to be honest, those of us with decades of experience in fitting are *still* learning. So, you need to find a clubmaker who is a skilled *club fitter*. We call these people professional clubmakers.

If you want to separate the wheat from the chaff, here are some questions you might ask if you're hunting in the phone book and you don't have any recommendations from fellow golfers. No, don't go in with a pencil and paper. Just sort of casually bring up one or more of these things when you're talking to him or her.

1. *How will you determine what is the best shaft flex for my game?*

Best Answer: I'll take a look at your existing shafts and ask you some questions about your experience and results with them; then I'll measure your swing speed and look at your swing to determine what shaft weight, flex, and flex distribution (tip flexibility, butt flexibility, bend profile, etc.) are best matched to your swing and how you play.

Good Answer: I'll measure your swing speed and compare that to information I have about the swing speed requirement of various shafts I may have in mind for your game. Then I'll talk to you about the different options for different shot height and feel within these shafts that match your swing speed.

The "Walk Away" or "Hang Up the Phone" Answer: I'll watch you hit some shots and I'll know from my experience what flex you need. Or, I'll check your clubs and see what you play and decide from that.

2. What can you do to correct my accuracy problem with the driver?

Best Answer: I'll watch your ball-striking results on my swing computer/launch monitor to see your primary misdirection problem and how much the face is open or closed at impact. Then I'll ask you some questions about whether you hit the driver off line and by how much. I'll check your current driver to see whether its specifications are appropriate for what I see in my measurements and observations. I'll also check you carefully for the right driver length, shaft weight, flex, swingweight, and grip size and, from that, make a recommendation for the best driver face angle, offset hosel or not, length, total weight, swingweight, and grip size.

Good Answer: I'll ask you about the direction in which you miss the ball most often and talk to you about a different driver face angle. I'll also see what is the best length and swingweight for you to be able to hit the ball straighter.

The "Walk Away" or "Hang Up the Phone" Answer: Well, you probably need lessons to hit the ball more accurately, but stop by and I'll take a look and see.

3. What are some of the things you might be able to do to help me hit the driver farther?

Best Answer: I'll put you on our swing computer/launch monitor and measure things like your swing speed, launch angle, spin rate. Then I'll check your current driver for its specifications of loft, length, shaft weight, flex, and swingweight to see how well they fit you. In all likelihood, you might be playing a driver that is too long, has too little loft, or might be too stiff in the shaft, or the swingweight is off.

Good Answer: I will work with you on the proper loft, length, shaft, and swingweight because many golfers use clubs that are too long and have too little loft to achieve their maximum distance. Or, a little of this answer plus ... I can fit you into the driver that you can hit the farthest for your swing speed and ability.

The "Walk Away" or "Hang Up the Phone" Answer: I can build you a longer driver, and you might get a little more distance (or the person asks you what loft you are currently playing, you respond with a number lower than 10.5, and the person recommends a LOWER loft for more distance with the driver).

That's great, but where do I find these people? I mean, you don't exactly see a custom club shop on every street corner.

You've got that right. In fact, given the number of golfers, there should be far more trained clubmakers than there are. But they're out there. A professional clubmaker may operate from a rent-paying retail shop, or possibly work from their home, but don't let the location fool you. I know of many expert clubmakers who work in both retail and home shops as well as some not-so-skilled clubmakers who work from each location.

The best way to find a good one is to do what you do for almost every other product or service. If you see a golfer with a set of custom made clubs in the bag, ask who built the clubs and whether the fitting experience was worthwhile and enjoyable. If you get a positive recommendation, you're on your way.

The next thing you might want to look for is whether the clubmaker is accredited. There are two associations of clubmakers in the world today that offer clubmaker accreditation testing.

The *Professional Clubmakers Society* is the only independent professional association in custom clubmaking. The PCS is the leading organization in the field because, as an independent organization, their motives are strictly to promote the craft of professional custom clubmaking worldwide. Thus, if you have a clubmaker in your area who has achieved the status of PCS Class A, you will definitely be in good hands.

The other large organization of clubmakers is called the *Golf Clubmakers Association* and is operated by a large seller of clubmaking components. It exists as a profit-making center for the sponsoring company. However, as with the PCS, clubmakers who have passed the GCA's accreditation examination and achieved the distinction of Accredited, Professional, or Advanced clubmaker are definitely skilled in the craft. I know, because I not only helped create the first PCS Class A exam, I also created the GCA's accreditation program. I can tell you that the examinations of both these organizations are thorough and are a true indication of the clubmaker's level of skill.

Another way to seek the name of a competent clubmaker is through two different clubmaker locator services offered on the Internet. The Professional Clubmakers Society has a clubmaker locator link right on the home page of their web site (www .proclubmakers.org). Class A PCS members are identified clearly through this link. In addition, I have provided a Clubmaker Locator directory on the consumer web site of my company at www.twgolftech.com. All the professional clubmakers listed on my company's consumer web site are people whom I have either trained personally, or whom I have known for a long time in the craft.

Finally, I do not want to leave you with the impression that a clubmaker who does not have a PCS or GCA accreditation, or who is not listed through the PCS or my company's locator, is necessarily incompetent. Since the days of the original hickory shaft makers, club builders have been a notoriously independent and oft-times stubborn lot, and some are simply not "joiners." I know of a number of very skilled clubmakers who just plain don't feel a need to "pass a test to prove to anyone how good I am!"

What about the people who fit you at golf retail stores or golf course pro shops? Are they any good?

Some of them are, yes. But, I am going be brutally honest about this—they're few and far between. Generally, they simply don't receive or seek the training necessary to become as skilled as the accredited and/or highly experienced professional clubmaker.

Among the off-course retail golf stores, many simply do not offer true custom fitting. By "true custom fitting," I mean a situation where the clubmaker has access to a wide selection of clubhead, shaft, and grip designs and can build the clubs in-house to your individual specifications. Again, because the golf industry is starting to realize that custom fitting may present a good opportunity for increasing sales, many of the large off-course retail golf stores have equipped themselves with launch monitors and other types of swing analysis equipment. Some retail stores do have accredited clubmakers on hand. (I think they ALL should have them.) If so, and if they offer fitting from a wide selection of components, then that's great. As Allstate says, "You're in good hands." However, if the retail golf store offers to "custom fit" you from among their existing clubs with maybe only minor alterations, and puts you through a ten-minute session to fit you, then forget it. That's *not* true custom fitting.

Then there are pro shops. *Sigh.* This one pains me greatly because I started in the golf business as a PGA assistant club professional before I became totally consumed with design and fitting. So I definitely have a soft spot for the PGA club professionals. In my career, I have had the opportunity to conduct a number of clubmaking and club-fitting seminars for PGA club professionals and assistants. Most definitely there *are* decent clubfitters among the PGA professionals who do such a good job of teaching and administering the game. Most, however, simply do not receive adequate training, nor do they make it a priority to add real custom fitting to their repertoires. As a group they tend to impose far too many of their own likes and dislikes (i.e., the things that work best for their own golf game) in making equipment recommendations for their members and other golfers. Such pros tend to forget that YOUR game is likely quite different from theirs. I do hope that someday PGA professionals will really wake up and realize how woefully inadequate their training in club fitting is so they can improve and really become a valuable equipment advisor for their members and golfers in general.

But let's say I still can't find a clubmaker in my area. What about the Internet? Can I get a good driver there?

It's no secret that I believe any golfer, at any level, will benefit from custom built golf clubs. But I am also a realist; I know that not everyone will have access to a qualified clubmaker within a convenient distance from home. If you are in that position, the next best thing you can do is to take a look at purchasing from a qualified clubmaker *through the Internet*.

Let me be clear. Working with a clubmaker from afar is NOT as good as being able to work face-to-face with a skilled clubmaker in your area. That being said, let me also point out that it CAN be far better than buying off the rack. But you have to do your homework.

Growing numbers of professional clubmakers have chosen to offer their services through Internet web sites. Their methods are as varied as the clubmakers offering the service. Some ask enough of the right questions to do a good job in making a fitting recommendation; others don't. So, if you are interested in this option, I urge you to take the same careful approach you would take in selecting any professional clubmaker. E-mail and ask for references of other golfers they have fitted long distance whom you can contact and ask about their experiences and most important, results.

Take a look at the online questions they use to make your fitting recommendations. At a *minimum,* they must include the following:

- *Some request for your swing speed.* This can actually be in the form of asking whether you know your swing speed with the driver/3-wood or inquiring about your carry distance with specific clubs.
- *Asking you for your height and arm length, or asking you to do a measurement of the distance from your wrist to the floor.* From this measurement, the clubmaker might also be able to approximate the best lie angle for your irons.
- *There should be questions about your swing and how you play, as well as what you wish to achieve in terms of shot changes with a new set of custom clubs.* The more extensive these questions, the better the depth of information the clubmaker will have in making the right decisions.
- *There should be questions about what grip size you prefer, or a request for measurement of your hand size or finger lengths so as to try to ensure a comfortable grip size on your custom clubs.*
- *There should be questions concerning your current set* including those about set makeup, what is the longest club you hit with reasonable confidence in the woods and irons, as well as about what sizes or styles of clubheads you find acceptable.

- *You should at least try to satisfy yourself that the clubmaker is using top-quality components.* Sorry, but I am going to have to get in a gratuitous plug here. If they are using heads and shafts from my company, Tom Wishon Golf Technology, you are getting the highest possible quality (seriously). But I must be fair and point out that there are others who provide clubmakers with high-quality clubheads. You need to ask the clubmaker what brand of components he or she uses, and then do a little research to see how good that brand is.

Because the Internet is such a powerful communications force, things may change in the future when it comes to real custom fitting online. For example, there is a totally new form of fitting data acquisition that is just becoming available to clubmakers. Specially wired electronic clubs could be shipped to golfers who would then hit real shots with the equipment. These clubs would in turn log all pertinent swing information into a computer module embedded inside the shaft, under the grip. These "Smart Swing" electronic clubs would then be shipped back to the custom clubmaker, who would download the shot results and be able to make an accurate, real custom fitting recommendation. While the Smart Swing clubs are in limited use now, the power of the Internet and its ability to reach many golfers who otherwise would not have easy access to a good custom clubmaker might very well change the face of custom clubmaking.

So, it's time to stop believing everything I see on TV or read in golf magazine ads about golf clubs?

Precisely. You don't believe everything that's fed to you in any other area, so why would you do so when it comes to golf equipment?

Look, here's the bottom line. Most of the brand name golf clubs are well assembled, with very high quality heads, shafts, and grips. *But they are all made to one set of "average golfer"* specifications with very few custom options, few if any of them in the most important areas of length, lie angle, loft angle, face angle, shaft model, grip type/size, and swingweight. It is simply not possible to make and market a club that way, which will truly improve the game for all golfers (as the ads so often claim).

Most golfers are used to believing the best clubs are the ones they have seen on tour, in ads, and on TV. You have been carefully conditioned NOT to ask the question: "How could one size possibly fit all?" You have been taught to buy hybrid replacements for your long irons, without asking why you suddenly need those hybrids. You are told you now need to buy a gap wedge, with the club companies praying you don't ask the question: "Where did the 'gap' come from?" You have been led to believe that the clubs played by the pros on the PGA Tour have something to do with the clubs you buy in your local golf store.

For Pete's sake ... ENOUGH!

I understand that to go to a professional clubmaker will require a certain leap of faith. It's the same thing that happened to me when I first needed to take my car in for repair and found no dealer for the brand of car I drive in my little city of 15,000 here in the southwest Colorado mountains. I had to ask people for recommendations and then go talk to the mechanic to get an impression. But if you have taken the time to seek out a skilled clubmaker, you'll be okay. You will be in the hands of someone who has pride in his or her work and cares for your needs. That person will not buy junk. He or she will choose quality heads, shafts and grips from which to craft your custom made clubs. There'll be no substandard "knock-offs" in a real custom fitted set of clubs.

Besides being technically skilled, the other thing that all good clubmakers have in common is that they *care* about the golfers they fit and serve. They know that if your clubs don't perform, you'll be back. I can assure you, the only time they want to see you back will be: (1) to add more custom clubs to your set, (2) if you bring a friend, spouse, or kid to be fitted, (3) if you have taken lessons, gotten much better, and need to have adjustments made in your current custom set, or (4) if you want to drop off a bottle of wine or a box of doughnuts in thanks for what they did to help you.

I want to say this one last time because it's so important. *I truly believe that all golfers, at all skill levels, need to have aspects of their golf clubs customized. These very real needs will not be met by buying standard, off-the-rack clubs.* I am not alone in this belief. The true professional clubmakers whom I have trained, helped, or just gotten to know all have the same belief and passion for creating golf clubs that truly *are* better.

Take some time to find a good professional clubmaker in your area. If you do, and if you love the game as much as we do, you will never regret it. Your clubs will finally bring you more enjoyment than sorrow!

Part II

But If It IS Broke,
Why NOT Fix It?

5 Fixin' Driver Faults by Lookin' at Your Shots

Okay, I'll admit it. There is a lot more to the driver than I thought. And what you're saying is that my pro, I, and every other golfer can overcome our shotmaking problems by getting a club that is properly fitted.

No. That is not quite what I am saying.

Do you remember earlier when I said that there is no way you can buy your way into being a great golfer? There is a reason for that: *An atrocious swing will overcome the corrective specifications of a well-fitted club every time.*

Let's say you have a golfer who consistently pushes or slices the ball to the right. For whatever reason, whether it be swing path or opening the face with the arms and hands, the golfer is coming into the ball with the clubhead 2, 3, 4 degrees open. Now, as a clubmaker, I can correct that. I can build a club with a head that has a face that is 2, 3, or even 4 degrees closed. Thus, with the new club, when that golfer makes the same swing as before and hits the ball, the net effect will be that the face is square. Even if the golfer is arriving at impact with the face of the driver 5, 6, or 7 degrees open. I can't get rid of the curve of the shot, but I sure as heck can use face angle and hosel offset to get that curve greatly reduced, and in the process keep the golfer much more in play than before.

But, suppose the golfer's swing is worse than that. Suppose our hero is coming in with a clubface that is 10 or 12 degrees open. There is not a lot I can do about that. That bad swing will have trumped virtually all the technology and skill at my disposal, and the ball will still slice deep in the rough, in the trees, or out of play.

Now, perhaps by having had custom fitted clubs in the first place, the golfer might not have developed that godawful swing, and I am certain that if that swing were not quite so bad, I could help. But as things stand, all I can do is recommend lessons.

But how do you know which to do? In other words, at what point do you "get thee to a professional clubmaker," and at what point do you "get thee to a teaching pro."

That's a great question. Unfortunately, it's not easy to answer because it's a classic chicken-egg thing. Which comes first, swing improvement or custom clubs? I would say, however, that there are three rules of thumb you might want to use to help decide that.

- First, if you are a beginner, or a relatively new player, get your clubs custom fitted for all of the things that make the clubs easier to hit, like shorter length, proper grip size, lighter total weight, more loft, etc.; *then* take some lessons.

  The game is tough enough to learn under any circumstances, but it's almost impossible to learn on your own. Start by maybe taking some group lessons where you can learn the basics. But, before you do that, get a set of clubs custom fitted. At a minimum you need clubs that are cut to the right length, with appropriate grips, and at least an approximation of the right flex in the shafts. At this stage you do not need to have your clubs creating swing errors for you; you will make enough on your own.
- Second, if you are an experienced player with swing faults and you are *determined* to correct them with lessons from a qualified instructor, go take your lessons, then get your clubs custom fitted.

  The key word in the above rule is "determined." Do you really have the commitment and determination to see the lessons through to a positive change in your swing? Just taking the odd lesson here or there might not be sufficient. I remember a veteran teaching pro with a Ph.D. in biomechanics telling me that a major swing change, like changing an outside/in swing path to a square or inside/out path would take 10,000 correct repetitions before the brain, nerves, and muscles had permanently learned that new swing move. If you have this commitment, go ahead and take the lessons and work your tail off to cement the changes. Then, when the corrections have been made and they are (hopefully) a permanent part of your game, go see your custom club maker. He can then tweak your old clubs or build a new set that is appropriate to your new swing.

- And third, if you are an experienced player with a good, repeating swing (even though you have some swing faults), and you have no plans to see a teaching pro to work on them, then go see a custom clubmaker.

Let's say you are the kind of golfer who has had a certain set of swing faults for years. You've learned to compensate for some, but with others, you've concluded they are simply the way you play the game, and seeing a teaching pro is just not in your foreseeable future. If that describes you, then seeing a professional custom clubmaker is imperative. The clubmaker might not be able to iron out all of your problems, but I am reasonably certain he or she will be able to get at some of them. I can almost guarantee you that you will be much better off after having a custom set or custom alterations made, than before.

But that's where you lose me. I'll admit, the golf club is a complex object, but I still don't see how you, or any clubmaker, can seriously affect my game with equipment changes.

Let me explain it this way. *Many times, golf shots are as they are because the golf club is as IT is. And sometimes the shots are as they are because the golfer actually overwhelms all the game-improvement aspects of fitting with a faulty swing!* The two are inextricably tied together. But the corollary to that is this. By changing the characteristics of the club, you can change the outcome of the shot for any given swing.

If you were to give me any common swing problem, I could show you, step by step, how an equipment modification could potentially help. I am not saying you should substitute custom equipment for lessons, but if lessons aren't in the cards, a custom club or custom alteration should be.

All right, professor. I have a list of common problems here. You tell me what causes them and tell me how they can be fixed or at least helped by altering my club.

You're on. Fire away.

Let's start with pushed shots.

A pushed shot flies on a straight line to the slice (right) side of the target. It is most typically caused by an inside/out swing path with the clubface open to the target line, but square to the swing path. The number-one swing mistake that generates a push occurs when the golfer moves his or her head in front of the ball before impact. Number two is poor alignment in the address position—the golfer's feet and shoulders are aimed to the right of the target. Both conditions shift the swing path more inside/out or keeps the hands and arms from rotating the clubface back closer to square and opens the door for the shot to fly straight to the right.

The number-one swing cure for pushed shots is to get the golfer to keep his or her head behind the ball through the entire downswing and impact.

From a club-fitting standpoint, pushed shots could be caused by:

(1)   the lie angle being too flat for the golfer at the moment of impact;
(2)   the swingweight/MOI of the driver being too high for the golfer's strength, swing tempo, and athletic ability;
(3)   the driver length being too long for the golfer's swing athletic ability, so that he or she simply cannot get the club all the way back to square at impact;
(4)   the face angle of the driver being more open than what the golfer needs for his or her swing path and/or delivery of the clubface to impact.

A pushed shot is rarely the result of the face angle of the driver being too open for the golfer. Such a condition would typically cause the ball to curve in a fade to slice action rather than to fly to the fade side of the target on a straight line.

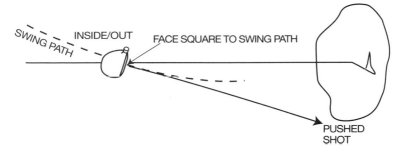

When the swing path is inside-to-out, and the face is square to that path, the ball will fly in a straight pushed shot.

OK, so how about the opposite, pulled shots?

A pulled shot flies to the hook (left) side of the target on a straight line. It is usually caused by an outside/in swing path, with the clubface closed to the target line, and a square to the outside/in swing path. The number-one swing mistake that generates a pull is when the golfer swings "over the top" and rotates the hands and arms around to try to deliver the face square. Another way to refer to this move is to think of the golfer swinging "across their body."

The second most common mistake that causes a pull is alignment—the golfer's feet and shoulders are aimed to the hook side of the target, which allows the club to be swung more across the body on an outside/in swing path.

The swing cure for pulled shots is to correct the golfer's alignment and retrain the swing path to be more square to inside/out by keeping the right elbow closer to the golfer's side, and making the golfer swing the right shoulder a little lower than the left shoulder on the downswing. (Left-handers, you know to reverse these, right?)

From a club-fitting standpoint, pulled shots could be caused by:

(1) the lie angle being too upright for the golfer at the moment of impact;

(2) the swingweight/MOI of the club being too low for the golfer's strength, swing tempo, and athletic ability;

(3) the face angle of the driver being more closed than what the golfer needs for his or her swing path.

Again, the pulled shot is less often the result of the face angle of the woods being too closed for the golfer. Typically, a face angle that is too closed for the golfer would cause the ball to curve in a draw to hook-ball flight curvature rather than to fly on a straight line to the left of the target.

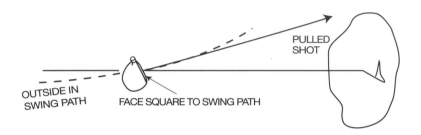

When the swing path is outside-to-inside, and the face is square to that path, the ball will fly in a straight pulled shot.

How about golfers who top the drive or hit the drive thin?

When the golfer tops or hits the ball "thin," the most typical reason is that the spine angle was straightened during the downswing. The next most common cause of the topped/thin shot is when the golfer straightens the bend in the knees during the downswing. The swing cure for topped or thin shots is to train the golfer to turn the hips and shoulders more on the downswing while working hard to maintain a consistent spine angle from the address position.

From a club-fitting standpoint, topped or thin shots could be exacerbated by:

(1) length being too short for the golfer to be able to maintain a consistent spine angle/knee flex;
(2) swingweight/MOI of the clubs being too low.

The reason I say exacerbated is that the clubs and their fitting specs are never going to be the main reason any golfer tops the ball. Pure topping of the ball is definitely a severe swing mistake that has to be cured by working to maintain consistent spine angle and knee flex during the downswing. Being aware of the golfer's comfort with the length of his or her clubs is not a way to prevent topping the ball, but it *is* a way to be sure the occasional topped shot and most thin shots do not happen very often to a golfer who does not normally top the ball.

What about the bane of so many of us golfers, sliced shots?

The ball will slice (curve to the right) whenever the face angle is open to the swing path at the moment of contact with the ball. A slice is most typically caused by an outside/in swing path, coupled with an open clubface. The more the face is open to the swing path, the more the ball will slice.

A slice can also be seen from a square swing path or an inside/out swing path simply when the hands and arms are not able to rotate the clubface back to square, so that the face arrives at impact open with respect to the swing path.

Because the slice is a very common misdirection problem, it is also important to discuss the variations of a low- and a high-trajectory slice. A low slice combines a downward angle of attack with an over-the-top, outside/in swing path and clubface open to the swing path. A high slice is caused by the face being open to the swing path while also traveling on an upward angle of attack to the ball.

The swing cure for a slice is to retrain the golfer's swing path to a square or inside/out path through the impact area. Just 10,000 correct repetitions and it'll be history! Trying to teach a golfer to rotate the hands and arms around a little more to alleviate a slice is very tricky and typically not a remedy pursued by many swing teachers. Thus, it is better to address the rotation of the hands' and arms' role in a slice by changing the golfer's grip to allow the hands and arms to swing as before, but to let the grip change automatically alter the hands' position so the face is less open to the swing path.

From a club-fitting standpoint, a slice can be addressed through:

(1) a change in the face angle of the driver to make it more closed than the face angle on the golfer's previous woods;
(2) a change to a driver head designed with an offset hosel;

(3) a shorter length, which can help reduce the amount of "over-the-top" motion at the beginning of the downswing;

(4) a higher-swingweight/MOI, which can also help reduce the amount by which the golfer shifts the club over the top and thus into a less outside/in swing path at the start of the downswing;

(5) possibly by a change in the weight distribution of the clubhead so that the center of gravity is slightly to the heel side of the center of the face;

(6) proper fitting of the lie angle to correct the lie from possibly being too flat for the golfer, although in a driver this is a much less common reason for a noticeable slice.

In the case of a low slice, the club-fitting remedy would require consideration of a higher loft, a more flexible shaft (for golfers with a mid-to-late release of the wrist-cock on the downswing), and a move of the ball position farther forward. For a high slice, the options are fewer because of the impossible-to-overcome effect of the wrists flexing forward on the height of the shot. If the golfer's high slice includes placement of the clubhead in front of the hands at impact, there is very little a clubmaker can do to lower the flight. But can you decrease the slice part of the high slice shot? Yes, definitely, with any or all of the above six methods.

And how about those golfers who hook the ball?

The ball will hook whenever the face angle is closed at impact in relation to the swing path. A hook is most typically caused when the hands and arms over-rotate the clubface past square, so the face arrives closed. It is far more typical for a hook to originate from a square or inside/out swing path, since the face only has to be closed a little bit to the swing path for the ball to curve in a hooking flight.

The swing cure for a hook is to retrain the golfer's rotation of the hands and arms by first trying to change the golfer's grip to allow the hands and arms to swing as before, but with the result of delivering the face less closed to the target line and/or swing path. Often, a grip change by itself is not enough to cure a hook, so it may also be necessary to teach the golfer to rotate the hands and arms less by training him or her to feel the hands in a more open position at impact, i.e., "keeping the right hand more under the left hand" through the ball.

From a club-fitting standpoint, a hook can be addressed through any or all of the following:

(1) a change in the face angle of the woods to be more open than the face angle on the golfer's previous woods;[1]
(2) a higher swingweight/MOI, which can also help offer the golfer a sense of resistance in the clubhead to reduce the rotation of the hands and arms;
(3) a heavier shaft to increase the total weight and to try to reduce the rotation of the body as well as the hands and arms, also helping to prevent over-rotation;
(4) with slight-to-nagging hooks but not a severe hook, a change in the weight distribution of the clubhead so the center of gravity is slightly on the toe side of the center of the face; and rarely, but worth mentioning:
(5) a correction of the lie angle if the driver is much too upright for the golfer.

In the case of a low hook, the club-fitting remedy would require any or all of the above as well as consideration of a higher loft, and/or a move of the ball position farther forward. Most golfers who hit a low hook could possibly do without some of the above five remedial changes if a more flexible shaft were prescribed.

For a high hook the options are fewer, again because of the strong effect of the wrists flexing forward at the height of the shot. If the golfer's high hook includes this placement of the clubhead in front of the hands at impact, there is very little a clubmaker can do to lower the flight unless the golfer is playing with too much loft by accident. Decreasing the hook part of the high slice shot can definitely be achieved using any or all of the above methods.

---

[1] Purchasing more open face-angle woods is very difficult in the clubmaking industry because of the old rule of supply and demand. Fewer golfers need more open face-angle woods, so companies are less likely to stock and offer such a specification in their product line.

What about hitting the ball too high?

When the golfer hits the ball too high with the driver, before anything else, first check the simple and obvious: determine whether the point of impact is high on the face or more toward the middle. If the impact is very high on the face, some relief from the problem can be offered, either in the form of insisting the golfer get used to teeing the ball lower, or by fitting the golfer into a driver head with a lower loft, or both.

On the other hand, if the golfer hits the ball too high and impact is consistently in the middle area of the face, now you have a little problem that an equipment change is not likely to remedy. No question, it is worth checking the golfer's ball position to see if it perhaps may be too far forward. If so, get the golfer to move it back and see if the change will make much of a difference in the height of the shot.

Unfortunately, if the ball position is off the left heel, impact is around the center of the face, and the golfer hits the ball too high with the driver, the cure is going to have to be administered by a competent teaching professional. The reason is that the golfer allows the wrists to flex forward before impact, which in turn causes the driver head to hit the ball on a sudden and severe upward angle of attack. This adds a lot of loft to the head as it hits the ball, and the golfer ends up with a very high trajectory, pretty much regardless of the loft. When this happens, the golfer has to retrain his or her release so that the clubhead will not pass the hands before impact, and the driver can be delivered to impact so the line from the forward shoulder to the clubhead is virtually straight.

If the ball position is OK, hopefully the golfer is using a head with too much loft, and the change to a much lower loft will have a significant effect on the height of the shot. But if the golfer is hitting the ball very high, in the center of the face of a 9-degree driver, you'd be far better off suggesting lessons to get rid of the swing problem that is causing the very high angle of attack than to prescribe a 6- or 7-degree driver loft. Swing fundamentals to address in this case are (1) retraining the release of the wrist-cock angle to occur later in the downswing and (2) teaching the golfer to turn and shift weight to the forward foot on the downswing.

Ugh, that sounds like a tough one to get over, so how about getting over the problem of hitting the driver too low?

There are several options for increasing the trajectory of the shot through club-fitting recommendations. Low shots are most typically caused when the golfer either swings the driver to the ball on a downward angle of attack, or straightens up during the swing and hits the ball very low on the face of the clubhead. Either way, it is possible to make much more impact on a golfer's trajectory with the driver than the other way around.

From a club-fitting standpoint, the golfer can increase the driver head loft as the primary solution. Remedies such as a more flexible shaft and/or a clubhead with a much more rearward and lower center of gravity will likely offer only a minor increase in the height of the shot, and only for golfers with a better swing, i.e., golfers who have a little later unhinging of the wrist-cock before impact. Loft is by far your best friend when it comes to helping the golfer hit the ball higher to achieve an optimum launch angle for maximum distance.

What about getting rid of hitting the ball off center, like when you hit the ball more off the toe or heel than in the center than you'd like?

While off-center hits more often than not occur when golfers move the head and upper body all around during the swing, a whole lot of that swing error can be stabilized by using a driver with a shorter length. Or, more specifically, using a driver that is fitted to the golfer's wrist-to-floor measurement, plus the golfer's swing tempo and athletic ability. Here again, I can't tell you how many custom clubmakers have increased a golfer's on-center hit percentage simply by cutting down commercial drivers to a length that is easier for the golfer to swing *with control*.

Next is the swingweight or the MOI of the driver.

In fitting numerous golfers, I see many of the heel-side hits alleviated with a higher swingweight or MOI (meaning more headweight) than before. But this almost always goes hand-in-hand with a shorter length.

For toe hits with the driver, there are a couple of clubmaking things to consider. First, if the golfer has a very strong transition and begins the downswing with more force than the average golfer, a shift to a shaft that has a stiffer flex and/or a bend profile design that is described as more butt-firm can reduce toe hits a lot. But if the golfer has an average backswing-to-downswing transition, this too has to revert back to a shorter length with the right swingweight or MOI to match the golfer's strength, transition, and swing tempo.

So, you see. There really IS a great deal that can be done to help you with your swing flaws, simply by having equipment that is thoughtfully built with your needs in mind! And you are NOT going to get that off the rack at Fast Freddy's Golf Emporium.

I gotta ask you about something I read about drivers in one of the magazines. With the move into big 460cc-size driver heads, with their taller faces, is it true that the "hot spot" for most distance is above the center of the face?

I'm glad you brought that up, because I read and hear that too from the various "mavens" in print and on TV and it just makes me cringe every time I hear it.

The reason that most golfers hit the ball farther when the face impacts the ball a little above the center is that that's the point on the face where the loft allows the golfer to achieve the optimum launch angle for maximum distance. Remember? Almost all drivers are designed with a certain radius from top to bottom on the face, called vertical roll. When you buy a driver with 9.5, 10, or any degree of loft, that loft exists only in the very center of the face, an area about the size of the head of a thumbtack. Due to the vertical roll, the loft will be higher above the center of the face and lower anywhere below face center.

Look, most golfers *do* buy enough loft on their drivers to hit the ball on the best launch angle for their swing speed and angle of attack into the ball. By teeing the ball higher and making contact on the upper half of the face, they actually are hitting the ball where there is 2 or 3 degrees more loft than there is in the center of the face, and from that they hit a better launch angle that will allow the ball to stay in the air to fly farther for their swing speed.

If you think of a "hot spot" as the place on the face where the ball speed is the highest for your swing speed, that point is going to be much closer to the center of the face than it will be on the upper half of the face. The absolute ideal condition for maximum distance with a driver happens *when you buy the right loft in the first place.* On the other hand, if you still use less loft than you should and you keep hitting the ball high on the face to get good distance, do me a favor and don't think of this as the "hot spot." Think of it as compensating for the fact that you should have bought a little higher loft driver, but still leaving yourself a tad short of the optimum combination I just described.

OK, so now that you've enlightened me about my driver, let me see if I can sum this up in common-sense terms. Above all else I need to make sure that the length, loft, face angle, and swingweight or MOI of my driver are all perfectly fitted to the way I swing, or else I can't hope to hit the driver as far, as straight, and as consistently as my ability will allow, right?

I could not have said it better myself. Wait a minute ... I think I did say so myself. But while you're at it, you might as well also get yourself fitted into the right shaft flex and shaft bend profile, and with the most comfortable grip you've ever wrapped your hands around to ensure that driver is going to make you all that you can be.

6 | The Right Driver for Your Swing

Address and Set-Up

I have a problem getting a consistent trajectory off the tee. I keep playing with the ball location, moving it forward or back, but nothing seems to help.

That doesn't surprise me. You see, every time you change the location of the ball relative to the lowest point in your swing, you change the loft of the club when it actually arrives to hit the ball. What *does* surprise me is the number of golfers who do it.

Most golfers are taught that the farther forward in your stance you tee the ball, the higher its flight path (trajectory) will be, and the farther back you place it, the lower its trajectory. Well, that's true in the sense that when the ball is forward of the lowest point in your swing, you will by definition be hitting it on the upswing, thus giving it more height. The problem is that it is not as true today as it once was.

In the good old days (i.e., only a few years ago), driver heads were not nearly as big as they are today. Their faces were maybe an inch and a half tall, as opposed to the two to two and a half inches of today. When they were smaller, the vertical roll radius of curvature on the face had little or no effect (see chapter 1); as heads got bigger, however, the influence of roll got bigger. On a modern driver clubface, if you hit the ball right at the midpoint, you will get your 10-degree (or whatever) loft, because in the engineering of all driver heads, that is the agreed-upon point for loft measurement. If you hit above it—if you are hitting higher up on the roll radius—you will get more loft. If you hit below it, you will get much less.

Thus, when you stick the ball up on one of those four-inch tees, and leave that ball perched way up there like one of the Flying Wallendas on a high wire, you are engaging in a crapshoot. You have no idea what kind of loft you are going to get until the club strikes the ball, and your guess is as good as your playing partner's as to its trajectory.

If you want a consistent trajectory, what you need is a club that is built to give you that trajectory each and every time you swing it. By verifying and choosing the right clubhead loft for your swing speed and your upward or downward swing through the ball (angle of attack), and by selecting clubheads in which the center of gravity is either forward or back, a clubmaker can predictably do that for you.

I can't emphasize this enough. *If you want maximum distance, the loft has to match your swing speed and your swing angle of attack.* Remember, the hose analogy we used earlier? If water pressure is low (i.e., your swing speed), you must raise the angle of the nozzle to get more distance. If water pressure is high (i.e., a higher swing speed), you get maximum distance by holding the nozzle lower.

Do not rely on a complicated process of teeing the ball at various heights, catching the ball in the exact middle of the face on the upswing, and guessing at what effective loft is right for you. Get a clubhead that has the correct loft for *you* in the first place, address the ball in one consistent location (i.e., slightly forward of the lowest point in your swing), tee the ball the height that will allow you to make contact where that correct loft is on the face, and have at it ... with CONFIDENCE.

The Backswing

One thing I've always wondered about is how you find, and then consistently apply, the right tempo to the takeaway and the backswing of your driver. Are there any equipment modifications that can help me with that?

Absolutely. And you're right in pointing out the importance of having a good backswing tempo. Have you ever read what Bobby Jones' swing teacher Stewart Maiden told him to jog him out of a ball-hitting slump? Maiden saw that the two halves of his swing were not in good synchronous tempo with each other, so he told Jones to "hit it with your backswing." The light bulb went on, and Jones' problem was solved. But let's start with finding the right tempo in the first place.

I wish there were a magic formula I could apply to this question, but there isn't. There are as many swing tempos are as there are golfers, and not all of those tempos are well matched to their owners. Some instructors will suggest you go out and observe other golfers at a driving range, watch their tempos, and try to settle on one that looks and feels right. Others suggest that tempo is tied automatically to the golfer's personality. The hard charging type-A personality will have a naturally fast tempo, so that's what he or she should use. The more laid-back person will have a slower, smoother swing.

All I can tell you is to experiment—that, and one other thing. I have rarely, if ever, seen a golfer whose backswing, especially the backswing with the driver, was too slow. On the other hand, if I had a dime for every golfer who jerked himself off the ball with a backswing that is too fast, I'd be playing golf at Pebble Beach right now, instead of working on this manuscript. So, if you are going to err, err on the slow side, okay?

But suppose you are possessed of a swing tempo that is simply not working for you, and that, try as you might, you cannot consciously change it. There are some things that can be done to your clubs to help you help yourself, and a smart clubmaker will take up those solutions, in this order.

The first thing to try is to increase the swingweight of your club By making the clubhead feel heavier in your hands, it will make it easier for you to consciously slow down your backswing. If you really are fighting your swing tempo, you will need an increase of three swingweight points and possibly a little more. No big deal. Any qualified custom clubmaker can do that. And you can even get yourself a roll of lead tape and experiment with it on your own by sticking strips across the sole or around the back of the driver head.

The second possible "slow down the tempo" remedy is to build the driver with a heavier *total weight*, which means using a little to a much heavier shaft than the one you're currently using. In a lot of ways this is the single most effective thing the clubmaker can do, but it contains a built-in drawback. The heavier the total weight of the club, the slower your swing speed will be on the *downswing* as well as the backswing. The slower the downswing, the less distance you will achieve. But not to worry too much there, because the slowdown from a heavier shaft will easily be offset if the heavier total weight allows *you* to slow down and start hitting more drives on center rather than over on the toe or heel where you're losing 5 percent of your distance for each half-inch by which you miss the sweet spot!

But tempo is only one aspect, isn't it? Don't you also have to worry about the plane of your backswing as well as the tempo?

Indeed, you do, and this is a great example of the trouble you can get into when you buy standard, off-the-rack, one-size-fits-all drivers. But let me start at the beginning.

The swing plane is the angle at which you take the club back, relative to the ground. The closer your hands are to the ground at the end of the backswing, the "flatter" your swing plane; the higher your hands are held, the more "upright" the swing plane. A flat swing plane will look to the observer like the driver is being swung around the body, whereas an upright plane will look like the driver is moving to the top at a much steeper angle. Hey, just look at the pictures to see the basic differences among a flat, normal, and upright swing plane.

In clubmaking circles, there is an expression in which a golfer is said to have "Tall Person's (or Short Person's) Disease." Tall golfers typically have a tendency toward a much more upright swing plane. This means they find hitting irons fairly easy because they're shorter than the woods, but have a devil of a time with woods because they're all much longer than the irons. Shorter golfers usually have a tendency toward a flatter, more sweeping swing. This means they find hitting woods easy, but irons are a real problem. Either way, their swing plane is a naturally occurring function of their body type, and the length of their driver is going to need to correspond to the swing plane to make sure the driver is easier for the golfer to control and swing down on the right swing path.

Now, let me ask you a question.

When was the last time you went in to a golf store or pro shop to buy a driver (or any club), and they asked you about your swing

The golfer's swing plane can be identified by watching the angle of the arms and the position of the club in relation to the golfer's head and shoulder at the end of the backswing. When the arms and club are closer to the golfer's head, the swing plane is considered upright; closer to the shoulder and the swing plane is more flat; in between is the normal swing plane. The more upright the golfer's swing plane, the less the golfer will be able to control a driver with a longer length, while the more flat the golfer's swing plane, the more the golfer *might* be able to control a driver with a longer length.

plane? No question that the golfer's wrist-to-floor measurement starts the driver-length fitting process. But from that start, whether the *final* fitted length of the driver is the same, longer, or shorter than what the wrist-to-floor measurement says is also heavily determined by your swing plane. With a few exceptions, the more upright your swing plane, the more you want to avoid a driver any longer than what your wrist to floor measurement indicates. Fitting a golfer with an upright swing plane with a longer-than-measured driver length, especially one who swings over the top and outside/in to the ball, is generally a kiss of death in the tee shot game.

On the other hand, if a player with the flatter swing plane is only average-to-below-average in swing ability, this by itself does not mean he or she should be playing a driver length greater than what the wrist-to-floor measurement indicates. Swing athletic ability is paramount when it comes to whether a golfer can play a driver length any longer than the length indicated by the wrist-to-floor measurement. Let me put it this way. If you've got it with the swing moves, you can go with the longer length. If you don't, you don't.

I have continually had problems with slicing the ball. Some-one once said it was because my "face angle" at the top of my backswing was off. What's that about?

I am sort of laughing as I read your question. The reason is that I used to make a lot of money off my friends with that face angle thing you just described. I used to bet my friends that I could tell if someone was going to hook, slice, or hit the ball straight before they ever started their downswing. They would, of course, jump all over that bet because they didn't know there was a trick to it.

It is possible to note the tendency of a golfer to hit the ball off line from a mistake in manipulating the position of the clubface during the backswing. By looking at the orientation of the clubface at the end of the backswing, it can be possible to identify the cause of the misdirection and, from that, work on changing the way the arms and hands swing the driver back to get rid of the clubface position being the cause of the errant shots.

All I needed to do was to focus on the position of the clubface with respect to the ground when the club stopped at the top of the swing. If the toe was pointed down at a slight angle to the ground, the clubface was square, and I predicted the ball would go straight. If the toe was pointed dead straight down at the ground, the clubface was open, and a push or a slice would usually result. If the face was pointed at the sky at the end of the backswing, the clubhead was closed and a hook or pull would almost always occur.

Now, I use the words "usually" and "almost" because this bet wasn't a sure thing; there are a lot of other factors that go into hooking or slicing a ball. But it was an example of a perfect bet. The system was accurate enough that a lot of dollar bills came my way, but not so accurate that my friends would stop betting.

It is also a perfect example of how you can get yourself into trouble with your swing and have no idea that it's happening.

Where the face of the clubhead is located at the top of your backswing is not something you can easily determine yourself. The club is behind your head at the crucial moment, and, unless you have eyes back there, you'll never see it. Turning around to look doesn't help, because the act of turning influences the clubhead position.

The only way you can tell if there is a problem is to have a friend (with quick eyes) watch your swing, to have a qualified golf instructor or clubmaker (with trained eyes) take a look, or to video-record yourself and play the video back at slow speed. Actually there is one more way that's easier on your schedule and budget. Swing in front of a window outside your house. You can glance up without disrupting your swing position much and see the reflection of your swing and the face position of your driver at the top of the backswing.

The hitch is that most people do none of the above, because it never occurs to them that a face that's "open at the top" might the cause of their shot-making problems. As a result, that nasty open face becomes ingrained into their swing, by which point it is difficult, and in some cases almost impossible, to remove.

That's where an equipment adjustment could come into play.

If your backswing is placing your driver head in an open position and you can't make the correction through lessons or a grip change, you can counter that by getting a driver head with a closed (hook) face. A clubmaker can fit you with a variety of different driver heads with "hook faces" built in increments from one-half to 4 degrees. So, let's say you're bringing the club in with the face 4-degrees open. A 4-degree hook face built into your driver will neutralize that. A 2-degree hook face will cut the slice in half. So will a driver designed with an offset hosel. The net effect is that the face will be much closer to square, and, all other things being equal, the ball will lose a lot of that ugly banana.

This situation also illustrates the maxim that you can't buy your way into a good golf game. If your swing is such that the head is coming in, let's say, 10-degrees open, then you are out of luck.

There is nothing any clubmaker can do to completely correct that. On the other hand, that 4-degree hook face will correct some of the problem, so at least your slice or push may only be in the rough instead of over the fence in someone's back yard.

The Downswing

So, you've now got me halfway through my swing. Personally, I've got a normal swing plane. My driver's clubface is open, but I'm now clued into the hook face angle or offset driver head, and I am in my typical three-quarter backswing position. I assume the downswing is next.

Right you are. But let's talk first about the different types of downswings we're likely to find.

Imagine two golfers teeing off. Both have the same swing speed as measured by an electronic meter. But when you look at side-by-side video recordings of the two, you notice that one golfer's clubhead consistently arrives at the ball before the other's. If their swing speeds are the same, how can that happen? The answer is that the golfer whose driver is arriving sooner is *putting more swing force* on the club than the other person. Sure, we can say that he or she is accelerating the club more or putting more torque on the club, but from a fitting sense, we're more concerned with how much force the golfer puts on the driver, particularly on the shaft, from the time the downswing starts until the ball gets smashed off the tee.

Among clubmakers it is said that there are only two kinds of golfers: hitters and swingers. A "hitter" has a very forceful transition at the end of the backswing, and tends to accelerate the club like mad on the downswing. The "swinger" accelerates the clubhead too, but the speed buildup is more gradual and incremental. This golfer's transition from the end of the backswing to the start of the downswing is a little less forceful and more fluid. Because the golfer is applying less force to the shaft at the start of the downswing, he or she reduces the amount of initial bending both on the whole shaft and on the grip end (butt end) of the shaft.

The point here is this. If you place a driver with a shaft flex and bend profile that is appropriate for a swinger in the hands of a hitter, that golfer will, in all likelihood, be very uncomfortable with its feel and will probably try to make adjustments in the swing to

The stronger or more sudden and forceful the transition move to start the down-swing, the stiffer the flex, the heavier the shaft, the higher the swingweight, and the shorter the club length should be to prevent the golfer from having problems hitting the ball solid and on center. The smoother and more gradual the application of force by the golfer to start the downswing, the more flexible the flex, the lighter the shaft, the lower the swingweight, and the more the golfer *might* be able to control a longer length to hit the ball solid and on center a high percentage of the time.

make the shaft feel better and, as a result, will likely be spraying the ball all over the course. The same thing can be true if a hitters' shaft fell into the hands of a swinger, not to mention the likely loss of distance that could result.

What's the difference between the shafts in the two drivers? Or rather, what *should* be the difference to make sure both get the right shaft?

The hitter, the golfer with the more forceful transition and the faster downswing tempo, will need a stiffer shaft and/or a more "butt-firm" bend profile in the shaft to resist the heavy load put on it both during the transition and the downswing. Without that extra stiffness, it is very easy to lose the feeling of control of the head, and if you do that, who knows where the ball is going?

The second possible club-fitting adjustment for the hitter is to create a driver with a little higher shaft weight or a higher swingweight. While most of the graphite driver shafts are designed to weigh in the area of 60–65 grams, there are many models that are offered in an 80- or 90-gram version just for these types of hitters. For example, a whole bunch of the PGA Tour players use the 85–90 gram version of the graphite shafts that many of the shaft companies produced in a 65-gram model. If we either use a slightly heavier graphite shaft or increase the headweight, the clubhead will feel a little heavier overall (from the higher shaft weight) or a little more 'head-heavy' (higher swingweight). For the hitter with a strong transition and fast tempo, that's definitely not a bad thing.

With a shaft weight that's too light for the hitter, the swing can become so rapid that the golfer's brain loses track of where the clubhead is located in space and time. If this happens, the brain will become confused with regard to the path the arms are supposed to take and exactly when it is supposed to release the wrists. It doesn't take a rocket scientist to figure out that the confusion does nothing for getting the head returned and square to the ball.

When should you go with a heavier graphite shaft, as opposed to a light graphite shaft with a much heavier swingweight to help collar that swing tempo?

This is where the clubmaker's experience in having fitted many different golfers and seen the results can work to your benefit. Typically, if you are "sort of a hitter" and not a full-blown "gorilla" on the downswing, you can usually do well with the 60- to 65-gram shaft and a higher-than-normal (D3–D5) swingweight to go with it. The Gorilla? Here's where the heavier shaft to boost the total weight (and no swingweight under D2–D3) is going to be the better fit.

Keep in mind that I am not talking about golfers with super high swing speed when I talk about the hitter with the forceful transition and ability to pour on the coal through the whole downswing. It's possible for a golfer with any swing speed to be a "hitter" in terms of using a more sudden and forceful start to the downswing and thus applying more bending force to the shaft. Remember, the clubmaker will be fitting the shaft flex to the golfer on the basis of swing speed compared to the shaft's swing speed rating, but with a little kick upward in that shaft swing speed rating to correspond to the forceful transition and downswing acceleration of the hitter. If the forceful, accelerating hitter has a 90 mph swing speed, we're looking for shafts that are rated in the 90–100 mph range and not lower.

The swinger's club should be the reverse of the hitter's. For example, he or she will need a shaft with a bit more flex in it. This is because less force is being applied to the shaft during the transition and downswing, which, in turn, reduces the amount of bending force on the shaft. This same swinger will probably benefit from a lighter total weight of the club, and from a more normal swingweight, in the D0–D2 range. The golfer's swing tempo and acceleration simply are not fast enough to call for fitting measures to slow them down, nor is the swing fast enough for the brain to get confused.

Let's say the swinger in my example here also has a 90 mph swing speed. In his case, the clubmaker will be looking for shafts that have their flex rated in a range from 80 to 90 mph because this golfer's smooth transition and gradual downswing acceleration are not going to put that much bending force on the shaft.

So, you see how it works? The 90 mph hitter puts more bending force on the shaft, and thus needs his or her shaft chosen from among those which are rated at 90–100 mph, which means more stiffness, while the 90 mph smoother-transition-and-tempo swinger is better off with a more flexible shaft that has a swing speed rating of 80–90 mph. The same delineation can be done for hitters and swingers with any swing speed as long as they're hunting for their best driver shaft from a custom clubmaker who has the knowledge and experience to know the swing speed ratings of shafts and how to apply them to the individual swing speed *and* swing types of different golfers.

That's fine, but my downswing tempo is pretty average, so my driver shaft will be chosen from among shafts with a swing speed rating where my swing speed will be right in the middle of the mph range. My problem is that I can't seem to stop "casting off" my driver on the downswing. Can an equipment adjustment help me there?

I know what you mean, because I see golfers with an "early release" all the time. "Casting the club off," which is just another term to describe an early release, is one of the cardinal sins of the golf swing. Let's look at what happens when you do that.

When you rotate your shoulders and turn your hips away from the ball, your lead arm (left arm for you RHers and right arm for you southpaws) and the shaft form an angle at the wrist. A good ball-striker will start the downswing with the shoulders, hips, or body. This allows the hands not to dominate the start of the downswing action. The trick is to keep that arm-shaft wrist-cock angle as long as you can, releasing your wrist-cock only at the last second. A properly executed delay is known as a "late release" and results in maximum acceleration and speed for the golfer's natural strength and ability being delivered to the ball. More clubhead speed equals more distance.

If you are casting the club and unhinging the wrist-cock early, your downswing move is completely different. The first move of

The unhinging of the wrist-cock on the downswing is called the release. In general terms (and from left to right in the photos), golfers can have an early, midway, or a late release of the wrist-cock angle during the downswing. Being able to identify each general type of release is important for fitting the best shaft tip section design for each golfer.

the downswing is made by pulling the club down with the hands and arms. This causes the driver to extend out away from your body, and that nice wrist angle I just talked about is lost. Two things happen after that—both of them bad.

First, the early loss of that wrist-cock angle causes you to come into the ball at a much slower speed than what you could otherwise manage. Second, once your driver starts wandering out there away from your body on the North 40, you'll have a heck of a time getting it back on the track it is supposed to be following into the ball. What usually happens is that the club never gets there, and you wind up with an outside/in swing path. And that, my friend, will cause you to pay a little visit to Slice City.

Here is the key point. A properly fitted driver will not get rid of your tendency to cast, but it can help make up for some of the ill effects. And that is what accurate club-fitting is all about. Yes, in a perfect world, the golfer would see a competent swing coach and work like the dickens to learn how to hold that wrist-cock angle until later in the downswing. But shoot, developing a late release is definitely one of the more athletic moves in the golf swing, and not all golfers can learn to do that. The same is true for several other moves in the golf swing.

Some fitting changes can help a golfer overcome an actual swing deficiency. For example, the heavier total weight or higher swingweight can help a golfer learn to control a fast swing tempo. On the other hand, many other swing errors require the golfer to unlearn the bad move. But in the case of many of these swing faults, a properly fitted club can offset the poor shotmaking results of the bad swing move and allow the golfer to play and score better and in the process make the game more enjoyable. And *this* is precisely why custom fitting helps average golfers more than it usually helps the very accomplished player.

When a golfer delays the wrist release to the last second and keeps the club in closer to the body, he or she is able to accelerate the club more and achieve a higher swing speed when the club smashes into the ball. While I promised that I would not throw all sorts of scientific terms at you, it's a scientific fact that an early release increases the load that the club puts back onto the golfer. By being able to hold that wrist-cock angle through the start of the downswing, the golfer gets less resistance back from the club, and his or her strength can generate a higher swing speed for more distance. We can make up for that distance loss somewhat by providing you with a lighter shaft with more flexibility. And we can reduce your tendency to slice by giving you a driver with a face angle more closed than the one you have now.

Well, actually, it's worse than that. In addition to casting, I have problems with my weight shift. I have a tendency to "fire and fall back."

Ouch, again. Another cardinal sin, but luckily another swing situation where fitting can overcome some of the shot-making deficiency that this swing mistake causes.

I probably don't need to tell you what a proper weight shift looks like. You watch the pros on TV and see it with every swing they make. That's where the golfer transfers weight to the front foot during the downswing and through impact. You can tell when this is done properly, because you can see a golfer finishing the swing with the belt buckle facing downrange, and you can see the toe of the golfer's back shoe down in the grass with the heel up and the sole pointing directly back. It's really a graceful and beautiful move.

"Fire and fall back" is a deprecating description of a golfer who cannot accomplish that weight transfer through a good turn on the downswing through the ball. The golfer finishes with the weight on the back foot and, in so doing, loses a ton of distance.

You can see the same phenomenon in other sports. For example, a football quarterback who can set, turn his shoulders, and shift his weight to his forward foot and deliver the ball is going to fire a frozen rope. If he's scrambling and has to get the ball away with his weight still on his back foot, unless he is John Elway in his prime, he's going to put up a lame duck.

Here again, a club correction will not eliminate the problem, but can lessen its effects.

When you fire and fall back, two things are going to happen. First, you are going to swing up on the ball more, and second, you will probably slice the ball with an outside/in swing path. To help you get some of that distance back, we're going to give you a driver with a lighter total weight, a normal swingweight, and a shaft with more flex in it.

To help correct the outside/in swing path problem ... well, I'd like to take that up as a separate problem because it is so common, and there are so many ways it can happen.

Fair enough. Then speak to me of swing paths, guru of mine.

I will indeed, grasshopper. Make yourself comfortable, and we'll start by finding out what kind of swing path you have.

The swing path is the direction that the driver travels on the downswing and through the ball. There are three basic possibilities.

The first is the *outside/in (or outside-to-inside)* path. This occurs when the downswing begins on the outside of the target line (usu-

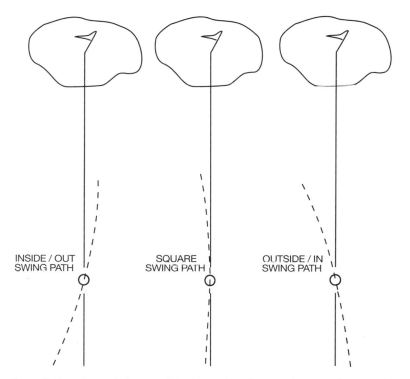

INSIDE / OUT
SWING PATH

SQUARE
SWING PATH

OUTSIDE / IN
SWING PATH

The golfer's swing path is one of the key swing elements that contributes to the accuracy and direction of the shot. It is also one of the most difficult swing moves to change. Golfers with an outside/inside swing path are more prone to slicing the ball and thus are better candidates for a driver with a more closed face angle and shorter shaft length. Golfers with an inside/outside swing path are more likely to draw or hook the ball and are then typically better matched to a square-to-open face angle on the driver, and *might* be more able to control a longer length. In between is the square swing path, which a high percentage of golfers would give up their firstborn child to possess.

ally because of "casting," or using the arms and hands too much to start the downswing) and travels through impact to the inside of the target line. The *inside/out (or inside-to-outside)* path is just the reverse. It starts on the inside, moves through impact, and winds up outside of the target line. If there is an ideal and perfect swing path, it would likely be the swing path that is *inside-to-inside* and, wouldn't you know it, it's the least common. This swing starts out on the inside of the target line, makes impact with the ball while the clubhead travels directly on the target line, and finishes again on the inside.

The problem is that it is not easy to figure out which you have. You can't actually see it yourself, so you have to have someone else stand behind you and watch. Unless the person is a trained observer of such things, however, it's still hard to see without a little cheating. The "cheating" I have in mind is for the observer to hold up a club, as if plumb-bobbing a putt, with the shaft along the target line. With this as a reference, the observer should be able to see your swing path without too much difficulty. Another way for you to have an idea of your swing path is to look at the direction of your divots with your middle irons. A divot pointing to the left for a right-handed golfer means an outside/in swing path. If the divot is to the right, you're looking at the results of an inside/out path. And a divot that is pointed straight at your target means you're probably one of the golfers at your course that the other players envy.

Let's say I have an outside/in swing. What then?

Then join the rest of us, because that is by far the most common swing path in the game. It is also almost a lead-pipe cinch that you are a slicer. If you're not, then you are overcoming that tendency by rotating the face of the club all the way around to pull the ball or, at the least, start the ball well to the left while you watch it curve back to the right.

In order to get that swing path you have to somehow get your hands and arms out away from your body during the downswing. Since the hands and arms are holding the club, the club will, obviously, shift over to the outside away from your body as well. Now, the club still has to hit the ball, and the ball is in a fixed position on a tee. Your brain knows this and does the most logical and efficient thing. It pulls the club back across your body in an effort to go find the ball.

At this point, one of three things will occur, depending on the angle of your clubface when it meets the ball. If the ball starts out to the left and then curves right in a slicing direction, the face of your outside/in club will be open to that line of your outside/in swing path. If the ball starts out to the left and keeps going straight left, then the face was square to that outside/in path. And if it

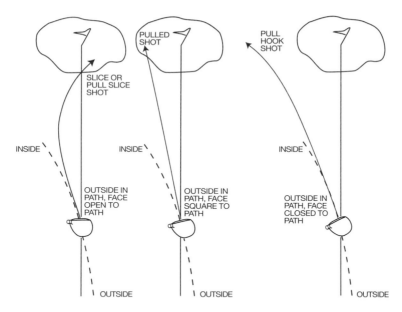

In reality, the swing path couples with the action of the hands/wrists/arms to determine the actual direction of the shot. In the example of an outside/inside swing path, if the hands/wrists/arms over-rotate the clubface to be closed in relation to the swing path, the shot will be a pull hook. If the hands/arms/wrists rotate the clubface on the downswing so that the face is square to the outside/in path, the result will be a straight pull. And if the hands/wrists/arms do not rotate the clubface enough on the downswing and leave the clubface open to the outside/in swing path, the result can be anything from a pull slice to an all out push slice, depending on how open the face is in relation to the swing path.

starts out left and curves even farther left, the clubface was closed to the swing path.

That is important for one reason. The only way that an equipment adjustment can help you is by changing the face angle of the clubhead or using a driver head designed with a fully offset hosel. Remember? An offset driver has the shaft and hosel out there in front of the face, so the golfer has a little more time to keep rotating the face around so it is less open at impact.

The rule of thumb is as follows. If you go the face angle fitting route, 1 degree of change in the face angle of the driver clubhead *over what you have now* will cause the ball to move approximately five yards less to the right or left at 200 yards of driver carry distance. So, if I see that you are slicing the ball 20–25 yards, I know that a driver with a 4-degree hook (closed) face will pretty much correct your slice or at least reduce much of its nastiness. Or, for the golfers who don't want to look at that much of a closed face angle on their driver, a driver with an offset hosel can also reduce the slice and get the ball back into play more often. So once again, sure, it would be nice to think that all golfers with an outside/in swing path would take the lessons and spend the time practicing to hit the 10,000 shots the biomechanics dudes say is required to ingrain the new swing path. But that doesn't happen that often, so here stands proper club fitting as a way to offer these golfers better shot results and more enjoyment of this great game.

So, what happens with an inside/out swing path?

The concepts here are the same as with the outside/in swing, but the causes and results are different.

Either dropping the hands and arms straight down, or moving them closer to the body, at the beginning of the downswing, causes an inside/out swing path. In that, again, the club drops to the inside of the target line before it swings out away from the body. Eventually, if you pulled that club deep inside the moment you started the downswing, at impact it crosses to the outside of the target line, and you get to stand back and admire your lovely snap-hook.

Once again, a good custom club maker can help you reduce and possibly eliminate the worst effects of this swing flaw with a face angle change, but the clubmaker still has to determine how much and in which direction. But unlike the slice, where the clubmaker has face angle and an offset hosel design with which to attack the malady, with the hooker we have only face angle to work with to really corral that duck.

If the ball starts out to the right and curves further right, your clubface is open with respect to that inside/out swing path. If it starts out right and continues straight right, the face is square; and if it starts right and curves left, it is closed in relation to the inside/out path. As with the outside/in swing path, the problem can be reduced, if not cured, by a change in the clubface angle. If a clubhead is 1-degree open (or closed), it will move the ball about

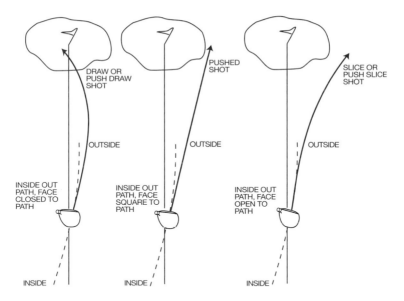

In the example of an inside/outside swing path, if the hands/wrists/arms over rotate the clubface to be closed in relation to the swing path, the shot will be a draw to a duck hook, depending on how closed the clubface is to the inside/out path. If the hands/arms/wrists rotate the clubface on the downswing so that the face is square to the inside/out path, the result will be a straight push. And if the hands/wrists/arms do not rotate the clubface enough on the downswing and leave the clubface open to the inside/out swing path, the result will be a pushed slice that most likely will mean "lost ball" or "OB."

5 yards different in sideways flight on a 200-yard drive. A 2-degree open driver face angle can make up for as much as 10 yards of a hooking mistake.

And if I should develop a nice inside-to-inside swing, I should apply for my PGA Champions Tour card?

Well, maybe not quite yet, but you might consider sending in an application to next year's championship tournament at your club.

When the driver travels from inside the target line, to impact, to inside the target line again, you have the perfect swing path. On the other hand, this is golf where we all know it ain't *how* as much as it is *how many*, so yes, you can admire an inside-inside path, but don't lose sleep over not having one as long as you are getting the most out of your ability and having fun while you whack it around.

Inside/in means your shoulders and arms are moving back down to the ball on pretty much the same plane that they took during the backswing, and your arms are staying right in front of your body through the entire swing. The result will be a ball that is hit straight, with maybe a slight draw or a little fade depending on the face angle of the driver being used.

And that ... is heaven.

So the bottom line is this. Proper fitting won't cure the swing mistakes we all have, but they sure can make living with them a whole lot easier and less stressful. After all, when you head home from the links, isn't life good when you have played better?

7 | Of Rookies and Retrofitting

It is no secret that I am a passionate advocate for the idea that all golfers should have their clubs custom built to complement each golfer's individual swing moves. I am not alone in this belief. In a recent television interview Tiger Woods was asked, "What is the most important thing that amateurs need to know about equipment these days?" He replied, "Proper fitting. I see so many amateurs I play with in Pro-Ams whose clubs are simply not fitted well to their swing. I think the ultimate key is to have the golf club fit you, not to try to fit yourself to the club."

There are two groups, however, for whom this message is a tough sell—and for very different reasons. The first is the beginning or high-handicap golfer (I am going to use the terms interchangeably here) who is sure that custom golf clubs are only for the advanced player. The second is the golfer who just spent something approaching the national debt of a third-world country on a set of the latest and greatest. He really does *not* want to hear that his investment might have been in vain.

I'd like to close this book with a special message to both of those groups. Specifically, to the beginner: *get thee to a clubmaker,* and here's why. To the experienced player with the shiny new set: all of that investment may not be totally lost.

Beginner Blues

As a beginner, it's pretty easy for you to believe that custom clubs are not for you. All you probably need to do is think back to your last trip to the driving range.

Now, I am not going to kid you; golf *is* a tough game to learn. Developing any type of repeating swing that consistently gets the ball well up in the air and within a landing zone 50 or 60 yards wide downrange requires a lot of practice and repetition. Learning how to move the club with your body playing a major role in the swing, without your body moving all over the place, is a tough skill to master. It's ballet with a stick in your hand! But, at the same time, you need to realize that hitting a golf ball is made a lot *more* difficult if the clubs don't fit you.

Would you attempt to compete in a track event wearing galoshes? Would you play football with a helmet that swivels around your head? Would you attempt to learn tennis with a badminton racket? No, you wouldn't. In fact, in any other sport, the *first* thing you'd do would be to make sure you had the proper equipment and that the equipment fit you. If that's that case, then why would you attempt to learn golf with a set of galoshes-thumping, helmet-swiveling, racket-swishing golf clubs?

Now, I am not saying you need to go out and buy a $1,200 set of pro-line beauties off the rack—just as you would not necessarily buy the most expensive track shoes or tennis racket right off the bat. You don't need to do that. In most cases, for the same amount of money—or less—you can get a reasonable set of golf clubs that will not actively prevent you from learning and enjoying the game.

Here's what a custom clubmaker can do for you, *even as a beginner*.

First on the list will be to make sure that your set make-up complements your ability. Thus, a typical new set for a beginning male golfer would be: a higher-lofted and shorter-length driver, 5-wood, 7-wood (or equivalent-distance-getting hybrid), then 6-iron through pitching wedge, and a sand wedge in place of the 5-iron. For the beginning female golfer, a good set makeup might be: a high-lofted and shorter driver, 5-wood, 7-wood (or hybrid), a 9-wood (or hybrid), then 7-iron through pitching wedge, and a sand wedge in place of the middle irons. Both of those sets would help make learning the swing a little easier and allow swing consistency to be achieved sooner. The longer and lower-lofted clubs can easily be added later after you have developed more consistency in your swing.

But do you see the point here? These sets would not cost one penny more than those you would buy off the shelf, yet the difference in the curve necessary to learn them is huge. This is the kind of flexibility of choice that clubmakers can offer, that already assembled club companies who fill the retail racks with standard sets of driver, 3- and 5-woods and 3- through pitching wedge irons can't.

But that's just the beginning.

Second has to be the length of the clubs. There is no question in my mind that the number-one problem with the clubs most beginners and high handicappers try to use is club length. Men who are beginners or high handicappers should not use a driver longer than 43 inches, with all the other fairway woods dropped in one-inch increments from that. Measuring for proper club length takes less than a minute and any custom clubmaker would be happy to do it for you. The maker needs that information to know how long to build your proper club lengths. Now compare that with the fact that most retail stores would be happy to sell you and everyone else sets of clubs of the same length.

And the list does not end there. A qualified clubmaker can make sure that the total weight and swingweight relationship in the clubs is set up properly. You can be sure the clubheads will have the right loft and lie angles. The clubmaker can make sure that the shaft flex is at least an approximation of the correct one for your swing, and make sure your clubs have the correct grips.

These are all things that most retail golf shops cannot (or will not) do, but that are done routinely, at no extra charge, by a qualified golf club maker. And every single one of those changes will make the game easier for you to learn.

Retrofitting for the Perplexed

OK, so you've read this book, seen the light, smacked yourself up alongside the head, and said, "Why didn't I have the set I just bought custom made?"

Well, that's a good question. There is no doubt that a set of custom built clubs would have been a better option. But all is not lost. Have you ever heard of retrofitting?

Retrofitting is where you undergo the same fitting process as with a true custom built set, but, instead of having your clubs built from scratch, your current set is modified to fit those parameters as closely as possible.

How close is "as closely as possible?" It's not as good as a true custom job, and depending on what your shot-making problems are, it may not really bring about that much improvement, but it's not a waste of time and money, either.

Obviously any grips that don't fit you can be replaced. Shafts that are of inappropriate lengths can be cut down or extended. Shafts that are of the wrong flex, weight, and bend profile design can be replaced. Clubs that are the wrong swingweight can be corrected, and iron heads and wedges that are the wrong loft or lie can be bent until they are right for you.

The one place where the news is probably going to be bad is with your driver head.

The head on a custom built driver is very, *very* carefully selected by a clubmaker. The loft must be correct for your swing speed and your swing angle of attack; the face angle must be correct for your misdirection swing tendencies, and so forth. The thing is, these are all variables that are determined by the design and casting of the head; they can *not* be changed later on. So, with the driver, you are a tad out of luck.

Will all these changes cost you a bit more money? Yes, they will, because they signal the need for a completely different driver head than what you probably bought. But hey, it's not like you don't get your money's worth from a driver in terms of how many times you have to hit it compared to most of the other clubs in your bag! On the other hand, it will allow you to make the acquaintance of a really neat person—your local professional clubmaker—so the next time you need a set of clubs, or need to know the truth about the next latest and greatest design technology that appears in the game, you know where to go.

Besides, if nothing else, it beats trying to play golf with the world's most expensive set of garden tools.

Afterword

One Final Word (well, maybe two or three!)

I love this game. I mean, I *really* love this game. I have ever since the first 9-hole round I played with my dad after a winter of indoor lessons when I was in the seventh grade. My fascination with the equipment of the game began when I was a senior in high school, and one of the local pros in my hometown taught me how to install new grips on my clubs. Shortly after that, I *knew* that I had to figure out a way to become a golf club designer. Despite the fact that such career positions don't exactly grow on trees, I dug and fought my way through self-training, formal study, and on-the-job training until I was able to get my first opportunity to start designing and doing research and testing of golf clubs when I was 30. I'm 55 now, and while I am so pleased that I have been able to learn what I have learned and do what I do, I am still just as fascinated with learning everything possible about the function and use of golf clubs as I was decades ago.

In short, you can call me one of the lucky ones. I realize how fortunate I am to have discovered something I truly love to do, and then to be able to make it my life's work. I've had the chance to learn more about golf clubs and their use than any other person in the game. I've had the chance to create golf clubs that have been used to win on the PGA Tour and in Ryder Cup competition, and I have had the opportunity to be able to create many different new "firsts" in golf club design. Only in America, as they say.

If you can't tell by now, I am absolutely positive that the best set of golf clubs *every golfer* will ever play will be a set that is accurately custom fitted and individually built for each golfer's individual swing and playing characteristics. That's not new. I actually realized that for the first time over twenty years ago, which is the reason I have plied my trade only within the custom clubmaking side of the golf industry.

In 2002, I turned down a chance to head up all design for one of the largest golf club companies in the world because I could not shake the thought that all I would be doing would be to keep putting standard-made, one-size-fits-all golf clubs on the racks of retail golf stores and pro shops. Believe me, that was a pretty tough decision. A seven-figure R&D budget, a staff of 30 or so engineers to do my bidding, numerous endorsement contract tour pros with whom I would work, and on top of all that, a mid-six-figure salary to do the "job." But I could not do it, because in my thirty-some years of doing what I do, I had learned above all else that golf clubs have to be truly custom fitted to allow any golfer to play to the best of his or her ability. I had also come to a point where I truly began to feel sorry for the millions of golfers who spend a lot of money trying to get the best clubs because of their love of the game, but fall short of that goal simply because they did not know the truth about what they really do need to play their best.

Once I mustered up the courage to say "thanks, but no thanks" to the offer, it was then that I knew I wanted to use the rest of my working life to do whatever I could to help golfers realize that there is a better alternative for getting the most for your golf equipment dollars. Personally, nothing frosts my butt more than when I go spend a bunch of money for something I didn't really know all of the facts about, only to find out later that what I bought did not fulfill all of my expectations because I did not find out everything I needed to know before pulling the trigger on the purchase.

Good golf clubs are not cheap. Heck, for that matter, cheap golf clubs are not all that cheap either, at least in terms of actual dollars. Since deciding to chuck the big salary positions and go it on my own to educate golfers about their clubs, my current salary is less than one-quarter of what it was in my position before I began doing my own thing. That means anything that is going to cost me a couple of hundred dollars or more is something that I darn well want to know is the best it can be for whatever purpose I have for the purchase. When I think about millions of golfers walking into large retail golf stores and forking over $1,000 to $2,000 for a new set of golf clubs, only to walk away with something that I know is not going to give them the most performance for their swing or for their money, it really bothers me. I think about how I would feel if I had ended up being a dentist with tons of knowledge about teeth, no more knowledge about golf clubs than you have, and a love for playing this great game—and I was in the market for a new set of clubs.

One thing that I have enjoyed in my career is teaching people who are interested everything possible about golf clubs. As I mentioned before, since 1981 I have taught over 200 clubmaker training programs/schools, and more than 2,500 clubmakers who came to these sessions because they too were interested in learning everything they could about golf clubs and club-fitting. I've come to really enjoy what I now call the "gee whiz effect," in other words, being able to tell people something about golf clubs that they did not previously know and that they found helpful and interesting.

Now that I am trying to expand my teaching to include as many regular golfers as possible, I have had the pleasure of hearing from many golfers who read the first book in this series, *The Search for the Perfect Golf Club,* and experienced their own form of "gee whiz effect" from reading what I have to tell them about their golf clubs. I've also come to the point where I get as big of a charge from that as I do from creating a new clubhead or shaft design, or discovering something I did not previously know about club-fitting.

Believe me, I don't have any axes to grind when it comes to the big companies that have chosen to make and sell standard golf clubs. They do a very good job in engineering the component heads, shafts, and grips that are assembled into their finished golf clubs. I just simply believe—no, let me say, I *know* that there is a better way, and I want to do what I can to get the message about custom fitting to as many golfers as I can. See, to me, the greatest discoveries happen when I find a different way to get to an end result that is truly better than a previous means that I had felt was the best procedure. In regard to the goal of matching the golfer with golf clubs that will enable him or her to get the most from abilities brought to the golf course, custom fitting is that "different way that is truly better."

I didn't write *The Search for the Perfect Golf Club* or this book just to push you into heading to your local clubmaker's shop to be custom fitted with a set of clubs that are of my design. Sure, I am proud of what I design and I truly believe it's the best. But heck, of the many golfers who have read the *Search* book and decided to be custom fitted, a whole lot of them have been fitted into designs made by some other company.

When I chucked the big salary and decided to do my own thing, I decided to do it in a little city of only 15,000 people in the mountains of southwest Colorado, about as far away from the "madding crowds" as one can be. So I am a little different person than most, with a very different idea now of the definition of success and happiness. I may be poorer than I used to be in a financial sense, but I also know that by pursuing my passion to teach all golfers more about their clubs, I am a whole lot richer than I have ever been before.

Above all, thanks for your interest in your golf clubs. I hope you've enjoyed learning a little more about your driver, and if all goes well, I'll see you again in the not-too-distant future when we talk in more detail about your putter. Goodness knows how important that club is to increasing your enjoyment in this great game!

Coming in

October 2007

*The Search
for the Perfect Putter*